SPACE EXPLORATION

◢ by Liz Kruesi

Content Consultant

Mary Kay Hemenway, PhD
Astronomy Department
University of Texas at Austin

Essential Library

An Imprint of Abdo Publishing | abdopublishing.com

CUTTING EDGE
SCIENCE +
TECHNOLOGY

abdopublishing.com

Published by Abdo Publishing, a division of ABDO, PO Box 398166, Minneapolis, Minnesota 55439. Copyright © 2016 by Abdo Consulting Group, Inc. International copyrights reserved in all countries. No part of this book may be reproduced in any form without written permission from the publisher. Essential Library™ is a trademark and logo of Abdo Publishing.

Printed in the United States of America, North Mankato, Minnesota
092015
012016

THIS BOOK CONTAINS
RECYCLED MATERIALS

Cover Photo: NASA
Interior Photos: ESA/Getty Images, 4–5, 7; Rex Features/AP Images, 9; NASA, 13, 22, 24, 26–27, 29, 31, 33, 36–37, 40, 45, 52, 53, 54, 58 (right), 59 (left), 60 (far left), 60 (left), 60 (middle left), 60 (middle right), 60 (right), 60 (far right), 61 (left), 61 (middle left), 61 (middle right), 61 (right), 62–63, 69, 71, 75, 74 (left), 74 (middle left), 74 (middle right), 74 (right), 77, 78–79, 85, 86–87, 89, 91, 94, 96; Bill Ingalls/NASA/AP Images, 15; Ann Ronan Pictures/Print Collector/Getty Images, 16–17; Bettmann/Corbis, 19; Chris Carlson/AP Images, 43; Aijaz Rahi/AP Images, 47; NASA/Handout/Corbis, 48–49; Red Line Editorial, 58 (left), 59 (right); rps/ullstein bild/Getty Images, 66; BLM Nevada, 81; SpaceX, 82; John Minchillo/PromaxBDA/AP Images, 93; Mikkel Juul Jensen/Science Source, 98

Editor: Arnold Ringstad
Series Designer: Craig Hinton

Library of Congress Control Number: 2015945635

Cataloging-in-Publication Data
Kruesi, Liz.
 Space exploration / Liz Kruesi.
   p. cm. -- (Cutting-edge science and technology)
 ISBN 978-1-62403-918-8 (lib. bdg.)
 Includes bibliographical references and index.
 1. Astronautics--Juvenile literature. 2. Outer space--Exploration--Juvenile literature.   I. Title.
 629.4--dc23

                                        2015945635

CONTENTS

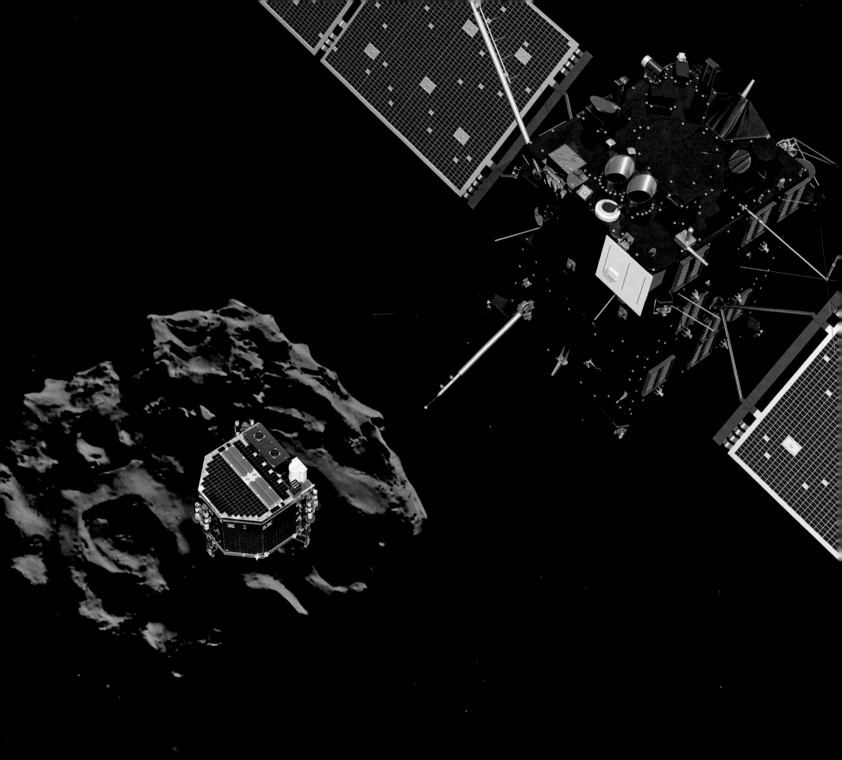

ONE

LANDING ON A COMET

On November 12, 2014, space scientists nervously waited in the European Space Agency (ESA) Space Operations Center in Germany. News would be arriving soon from their distant spacecraft, *Rosetta*. It was the first artificial object in history to orbit a comet.

Seven hours prior, the spacecraft released a lander to touch down on the comet below. If everything worked as planned, that lander, *Philae*, would be the first human-made machine to land on a comet. It would add immensely to scientists' knowledge about these icy, dusty space rocks.

Finally, the scientists got the news: *Philae* was on the surface of comet 67P/Churyumov–Gerasimenko, known as 67P for short. Flight Director Andrea Accomazzo wiped tears from his eyes following the good news.

In November 2014, after a ten-year voyage through space, Rosetta finally arrived at comet 67P.

However, the landing did not go exactly as planned. Scientists had programmed a specific sequence of commands into *Philae*'s memory. These steps told the robotic spacecraft what to do as soon as it was near the comet's surface. First, it was supposed to use a small rocket engine to push it toward the comet. Then, the ship would fire two harpoons to catch the surface. Finally, as soon as it made contact with the comet, screws at the end of each of *Philae*'s three legs would embed into the icy surface.

Unfortunately, all three mechanisms failed. Because the force of gravity on 67P is several hundred thousand times weaker than on Earth, the comet could not keep hold of *Philae*. So the lander bounced, rising in a high arc from the surface for almost two hours. Luckily, it did not drift into space. 67P's weak gravity gently tugged it back to the surface, where the lander made one more small bounce before nudging itself sideways against a rock wall. Some of the scientists later joked that they had made not only the first landing on a comet, but the first three.

Philae's internal batteries powered its first 50 hours on the surface.[1] For additional power to make it through the next few months of collecting data, as was originally planned, it needed sunlight. But its resting position put its solar panels in shadow. That meant its ten instruments could take measurements and send data back to *Rosetta* for only a few days. The science team made the most of

As Philae *touched down, the devices intended to anchor it to the comet failed to work properly, sending the lander bouncing upward.*

this limited time. *Philae* took the first incredible pictures from the surface of a comet, measured the temperature at its resting spot, and tried to drill into the rock. It revealed 67P has several inches of rocks and dust on its surface. Scientists were unsure what the material below the surface was, but they could determine it was as dense as solid ice.

Although the *Philae* landing did not go as planned, it was a tremendous technological feat. Humans landed a refrigerator-sized spacecraft on a comet while both were traveling as fast as 34,000 miles per hour (55,000 kmh) at a distance of 280 million miles (450 million km) from the sun.[2]

On June 13, 2015, ESA mission controllers received incredible news. Data sent back by the *Rosetta* spacecraft was telling them *Philae* had woken up after months of sitting on the comet's surface without power. They realized the comet had gotten close enough to the sun that the lander's solar panels could finally generate the electricity needed for *Philae* to function. Astronomers were thrilled. *Philae* was now poised to provide exciting new data on the changes the comet underwent as it made its closest approach to the sun.

Keys to the Early Solar System

Soviet astronomers discovered 67P in 1969.

Why would humans want to visit a comet? These dusty, icy rocks come from the outskirts of our solar system, where the temperatures are so cold all liquids have frozen solid. Water and other compounds that exist as liquids on Earth are ice in this region. The cold, comet-filled region surrounding the outer solar system is known as the Oort cloud.

If a large object, such as an asteroid or planet, passes near the Oort cloud, the object's gravitational pull disturbs the comets it passes. Some of these frozen comets will be thrown into the inner solar system. As a comet nears the sun, our star's heat turns those ices directly to gas. Astronomers can observe jets of these gases escaping a comet's surface. The gases form a coma, or cloud, that cloaks the comet's nucleus, or rocky body. The gases also stretch out in the opposite direction from the sun in a long tail. Comets often also have a second tail containing dust. This tailed, dusty object is what people commonly think of when they think of comets.

Rosetta watched 67P transform as it heated up on the way to its closest approach to the sun in August 2015. That is one of the goals of this space mission: to study how a comet goes from a rocky snowball to a glowing ball with a gaseous tail trailing it across the sky. After nearing the sun, 67P will be

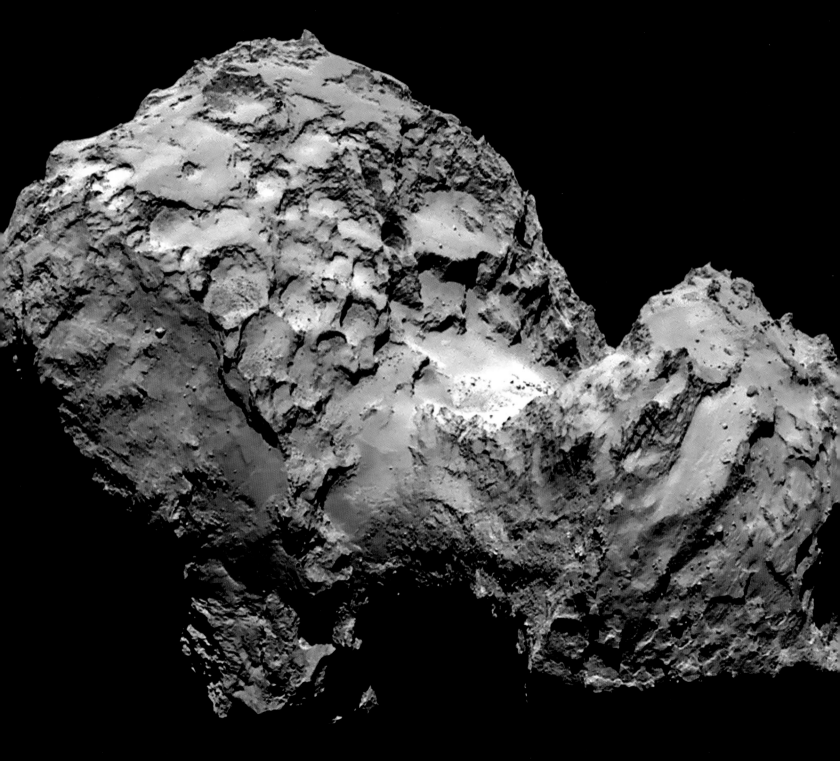

Visiting Other Comets

Rosetta was the first mission to orbit a comet, but it was not the first mission to visit one. *Giotto*, another ESA spacecraft, studied a comet three decades earlier. This mission's target was a more well-known comet—1P/Halley, better known as Halley's comet. *Giotto* studied this object during a flyby in 1986 from approximately 375 miles (600 km) away.[3]

Two decades later, in July 2005, NASA's *Deep Impact* spacecraft hurled a probe into Comet 9P/Tempel. The explosion gave astronomers an opportunity to study the comet's material. They found more powdery dust at the surface than expected. NASA also operated *Stardust*, which captured thousands of dust particles from Comet 81P/Wild in January 2004. The mission returned those samples to Earth two years later. The samples strongly suggested the presence of liquid water on the comet, contrary to the usual belief that comets never warm enough for their ice to melt.

flung out past Mars to the most distant part of its orbit. It will spend years drifting through space before it approaches the sun again.

Another major goal of the mission is to learn what materials make up those icy rocks. Comets come from the far reaches of our solar system. Scientists think that area harbors the same type of materials that made our Earth and the rest of the solar system more than 4 billion years ago. But the sun's light is faint where comets come from. That keeps the ingredients of the solar system in a deep freeze, hibernating for billions of years. Once a comet nears our sun and those ices melt, the space rock becomes a window to the early solar system.

Astronomers know the early solar system was a hectic place. Comets thrown from the Oort cloud were flying through the inner solar system. Some of them likely slammed into the young Earth. Scientists think comets and their closer-to-Earth cousins, asteroids, may have brought water to our planet billions of years ago. This water now fills the oceans, seas, and lakes, providing nourishment for life.

Rosetta has detected water, carbon monoxide, carbon dioxide, ammonia, methane, methanol, and nitrogen at 67P. Some of the comet's water, however, contains a different form of hydrogen in its molecules compared to the water and ice found on Earth. This means comets such as 67P could not have brought water to our planet. It is still possible other types of comets and asteroids could have dampened the early Earth.

Rosetta's Early Finds

Philae did not land until November 2014, but *Rosetta* first approached the comet a few months earlier. One of the orbiter's many discoveries happened in July 2014, once the craft was close enough to the comet to take clear images of it. Scientists were surprised to see 67P is shaped a bit like a rubber duck, with two large sections connected by a relatively narrow area. Astronomers had long expected it to be a simpler object, perhaps shaped like a rounded football or a loaf of bread. Scientists are still unsure whether this odd shape results from two smaller rocks slamming into each other or from one single comet that has been eroded away for billions of years.

Rosetta reached 67P on August 6, 2014. It then fired its engines to loop around the comet, entering an orbit approximately 19 miles (31 km) from the surface. Occasionally *Rosetta* would pass as close as 4 miles (6 km).[4] Since August 2014, the orbiter's 11 instruments have surveyed the comet, tracking any changes. After the landing, as *Philae* slept on the surface, *Rosetta* continued monitoring the comet. It watched 67P become more active as it neared its closest approach to the sun in August 2015.

Human space exploration is more dangerous than using robots, but many feel its potential rewards are worth the risk.

The Edge of the Unknown

The decades of effort leading up to the *Rosetta* mission have been an exciting journey, not only for the scientists involved but also for anyone who follows the news of cutting-edge space exploration. *Rosetta*, similar to many other space projects, has revealed new discoveries and led humans to the edge of the unknown. It has also raised brand-new questions about our celestial neighborhood.

Such endeavors are extremely difficult. Scientists have to account for many things that could go wrong. In space, stray dust particles could fatally damage a ship. Bursts of energy from the sun can damage experiments and harm any human occupants of a spacecraft. Not all risks are natural. Human errors can also threaten space missions.

Space missions constantly push humans' boundaries deeper into space. They reveal more about Earth's place in the solar system and the universe. And they extend our reach to more distant worlds. Humans and robots landed first on the moon, but now robots have touched down on more distant bodies, including Venus, Mars, an asteroid, and a comet. To get spacecraft to these places, humans push the edge of technology. Scientists and engineers develop huge, reliable rockets to blast spacecraft to their faraway destinations. The spacecraft themselves are designed to be rugged enough to survive the harsh conditions of space—and, if people are aboard, to keep a human crew alive.

The past 50 years of space exploration have seen both failures and triumphs. The perseverance of astronomers, engineers, and astronauts demonstrates the human commitment to extend our reach into the solar system. The cutting-edge space exploration that is being planned and executed in the first few decades of the 2000s will continue expanding and refining our knowledge of the universe around us.

Returning crews safely to Earth is one of the most challenging aspects of human spaceflight.

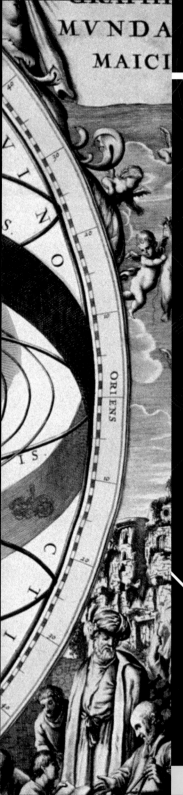

TWO

ENTERING
SPACE

A ncient peoples had many theories about the nature of the sky above them. Some thought the lights in the night sky were attached to different-sized globes, each one nested within the other, all surrounding Earth. The lights that moved fastest were closer. The ones that moved slowest were farther away. In this model, the moon was on the nearest globe, followed by the planets and the stars. By the 1600s, the work of several scientists, including Nicolaus Copernicus and Johannes Kepler, made it clear nearby celestial bodies traveled in paths around the sun, not Earth. These paths could be described and even predicted using mathematics.

Ancient astronomers had an
Earth-centered view of the cosmos.

17

After thousands of years of staring at the sky, people began developing technology to let them more clearly see faraway worlds. This revolution began in 1609, when two scientists—Thomas Harriot and Galileo Galilei—pointed early telescopes at the moon. The following year, Galileo looked to Jupiter and discovered its four largest moons. Then came observations of Saturn, Venus, and the sun.

Experiments aboard modern spacecraft have dramatically improved humanity's views of these distant celestial objects. But long before we had crisp images of these worlds, many people dreamed of what wonders space explorers might find.

◂ An Early Space Movie

In 1902, French filmmaker Georges Méliès directed *Le Voyage Dans La Lune* (*A Trip to the Moon*). This short black-and-white film has no sound. It begins with a scientist showing his fellow astronomers a plan to fly a rocket to the moon. Six of those scientists end up in a missile, shot to the moon by a cannon. Their missile lands right in the eye of the fabled man on the moon. Once on the moon, the group explores the surface and then travels underground. There they find a world alive with alien plants and creatures.

Space in Science Fiction

One of the most influential science fiction writers was French author Jules Verne, who worked in the 1800s. He wrote approximately 80 books and stories during his life.[1] Although his works included futuristic technology, many of these advances seemed feasible given the current experiments of the time.

One of his most popular works was *De la Terre à la Lune* (*From the Earth to the Moon*). In the novel, people build a powerful cannon to launch a spacecraft containing three men to the moon. Verne published the books in 1865, more than a century before humans first walked on the moon during the Apollo program in 1969. Yet many of the things he wrote about were

Verne's space explorers traveled aboard an enormous artillery shell.

later echoed in reality. Similar to Verne's travelers, the Apollo crews consisted of three astronauts and launched from Florida. Verne's powerful cannon was called the Columbiad; the Apollo 11 command module was coincidentally named *Columbia*.

H. G. Wells was another prolific author with grand ideas about space exploration. His ideas, however, were not as close to reality as Verne's were. Wells wrote of a journey to Earth's closest neighbor in *The First Men in the Moon*. But his mode of transportation, a glass sphere carried aloft in a fountain of air, was strictly fiction. Likewise, his story strayed from reality in featuring insect-like inhabitants of the moon.

Early Rockets

For the last half-century, astronomers have continuously studied our solar system using ever-advancing technology. They have sent robotic spacecraft to every planet, a few dwarf planets, many moons, and comets and asteroids. Even the sun has been visited. To get to these distant destinations, spacecraft need to be launched away from Earth at tremendous speeds. The only known machine that can achieve these speeds is the rocket.

A rocket is a cylindrical projectile that can be propelled to a great height or distance by the burning of its fuel. The exhaust produced by this burning is directed out the back of the rocket, pushing the vehicle forward. The earliest rockets were used as firework displays or weaponry. Historical evidence shows they first emerged in the 1100s. These early rockets were not capable of reaching space. Instead, they were fireworks that traveled along the ground. And the explosions that fueled those early rockets came about by accident. Chinese alchemists mixed together different forms of gunpowder and used them to launch weapons. It was not long before the potential of rocket weapons was recognized. Rockets remained as tools of war for centuries, although their low accuracy made them difficult to use effectively.

Toward Modern Rocketry

At the beginning of the 1900s, the use of rockets began changing. Russian schoolteacher Konstantin Tsiolkovsky wrote hundreds of articles about flying machines and the possibility of human spaceflight. In a 1903 paper, he suggested rockets could use oxygen and hydrocarbons as liquid fuels. This type of fuel would combust with enough energy to loft the rocket to higher altitudes than ever before. Such rockets would also be easier to control than the simple rockets that had been around for centuries.

American physicist Robert Goddard built the first rocket to use liquid fuel. Its first successful test took place on March 16, 1926. It climbed only 41 feet (12.5 m) and was in the air for only a few seconds, but the flight was still an important first step in the history of space exploration.[3]

In 1929, Goddard launched the first rocket with scientific instruments on board. For the next several years he also worked on new methods to guide and steer his rockets. He studied new ways to pump fuel into the engine. In 1961, the National Aeronautics and Space Administration (NASA) dedicated one of its centers to him: the Goddard Space Flight Center in Greenbelt, Maryland.

◢ Rockets for Science

The history of sending science experiments up in rockets began in 1929 with Robert Goddard's early work, when he launched a barometer and a camera. Modern researchers still loft detectors and other science instruments into the sky. Some study Earth from a height of thousands of feet, whereas others look down on the planet from thousands of miles. Scientific instruments that go into deep space may travel millions of miles from home. Instruments aboard rockets have been used for a wide array of purposes, including studying active regions on the sun, looking for light from the oldest galaxies, and learning more about the clouds in Earth's atmosphere.

Rockets of War

Scaling up Goddard's work into larger rockets would require a massive investment. Climbing military budgets during World War II (1939–1945) provided this opportunity, as Germany made rocket weapons a priority. Germany, controlled by Adolf Hitler and his Nazi Party, developed the Vergeltungswaffe-2

Goddard's work with liquid-fueled rockets laid the groundwork for all future space exploration.

rocket weapon, better known as the V-2. German engineer Wernher von Braun oversaw the effort to produce a rocket of 12 short tons (11 metric tons) that could carry a warhead weighing 1 short ton (0.9 metric ton).[4] The V-2 burned fuel at a rapid rate. Every second, its pumps forced 159 pounds (72 kg) of oxygen and 128 pounds (58 kg) of alcohol into the engine.[5] The combustion energy carried the rocket up to 220 miles (350 km) away, reaching a maximum altitude of 60 miles (100 km).[6]

Each V-2 rocket was set to travel a certain distance. Once it reached this limit, it stopped its fuel pumps and began coasting to its target. It hit the ground at faster than the speed of sound, far too fast to be intercepted or stopped. The explosion of its warhead leveled buildings. Germany launched more than 2,600 V-2 rockets at the United Kingdom and Belgium in 1944 and 1945.[7] The most casualties were in London, the densely populated capital of the United Kingdom.

After Germany fell and the war ended, the United States captured many German rocket engineers, including von Braun, and whisked them back to US soil. The scientists were put to work developing rockets for the US military. Captured V-2 rockets served as the starting point of many US space exploration developments.

◢ Brilliant and Controversial

Wernher von Braun was an integral part of NASA's space achievements. He was also a controversial figure. Before coming to the United States, he was a member of the Nazi Party and led the development of rocket weapons that killed thousands of people. The rocket factories involved the forced labor of thousands of concentration camp prisoners. After the war he claimed he had been unaware of the worst parts of Adolf Hitler's Nazi regime. Once in the United States, he became a US citizen and one of the top figures at NASA. Still, many people criticized him for his past work on weapons.

Toward Space

Von Braun and his team started their work at White Sands, New Mexico, in 1946. They began with leftover V-2 parts. The scientists worked to make better and more powerful rockets. They developed the Redstone rocket, which saw its first successful launch in 1954. A later version boosted the first

US rocket scientists collected
data during launches of
captured V-2s for use in their
research programs.

US satellite, *Explorer 1*, into orbit in January 1958. In October of that same year, the US government officially formed NASA.

But by this time, the Soviet Union had already gotten to space. The Soviet Union would later split into multiple countries, the largest of which is Russia. During the war, it had fought against Germany alongside the United States. But in the aftermath of World War II, the United States and the Soviet Union became rival powers. The United States had seized most of the German rocket scientists, but its wartime ally had access to German factories and leftover V-2s. They took apart the equipment to learn how to make their own rockets. And on October 4, 1957, the Soviet Union launched the world's first artificial satellite, *Sputnik 1*. This beach ball–sized spacecraft circled Earth in 96 minutes. The metal sphere carried a radio transmitter, a power supply, and a heating and cooling system. It weighed 184.3 pounds (83.6 kg).[8] For the first time, space exploration had left the world of science fiction and entered the realm of reality.

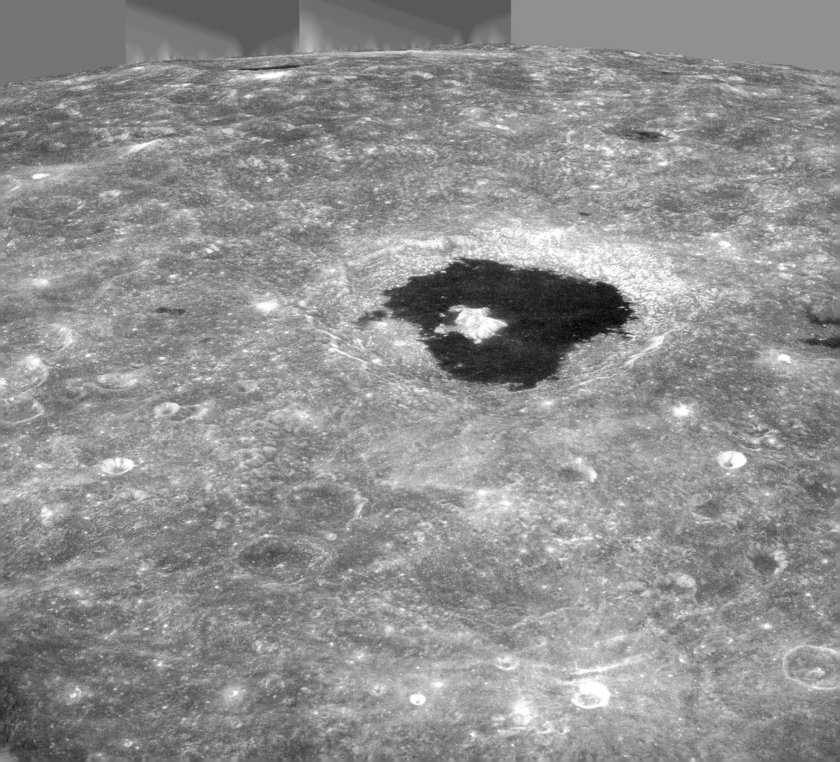

THREE

VISITING NEARBY WORLDS

Humanity's exploration beyond our own planet began with a mission to the moon. On October 7, 1959, the Soviet Union's *Luna-3* spacecraft captured 29 photographs of the far side of the moon.[1] The same side of the moon always faces Earth, so the far side had never been seen before. Onboard, the craft developed the pictures. On its return trip to Earth, *Luna-3* successfully transferred data of the images over radio link. For the first time in history, humans had photographs of another world captured by a spacecraft.

Luna-3 was among the first of many robotic explorers to embark on voyages through the inner solar system. Since its journey, spacecraft have studied Venus, Mercury, and the center of our solar system: the sun.

High-quality images of features on the moon's far side, including the striking Tsiolkovsky Crater, were later taken by crews on the US Apollo missions.

Earth is the best-studied planet of all. NASA's Earth Observatory program collects a vast number of images from many different studies of our planet. Some of these are global maps that show where fires are burning and how temperatures vary throughout the world. Others show rainfall and snow cover. Some of the most striking images are taken at night. These powerful photographs show city lights throughout the globe. They demonstrate how much humans have changed the planet.

Earth's Twin

Earth and its sister planet Venus are easy to tell apart. Both are rocky planets, and both are approximately the same size. That is where the similarities end. Venus has an extremely thick atmosphere made up mostly of carbon dioxide. This gas traps heat and does not let it escape. The result is a surface temperature of more than 850 degrees Fahrenheit (450°C).[2]

Years after the Venera *missions, the US orbiter* Magellan *used radar to build three-dimensional maps of Venus's surface beneath the clouds.*

The planet's crushing atmospheric pressure and scorching temperatures mean any spacecraft that lands there must be specially constructed to withstand the conditions. Only one space agency has attempted landings on the planet. The Soviet Union sent missions to Venus in the 1970s and 1980s. Several of its *Venera* and *Vega* spacecraft made it to the surface and sent information, including images and scientific measurements, back to Earth. They also collected data as they descended through the planet's dense clouds.

To land intact, the first two *Venera* probes used parachutes to slow their falls. Designers added aluminum heat shields and inflatable cushions to later versions. No spacecraft has landed on Venus since the mid-1980s, and by 2015 no future missions were in active development.

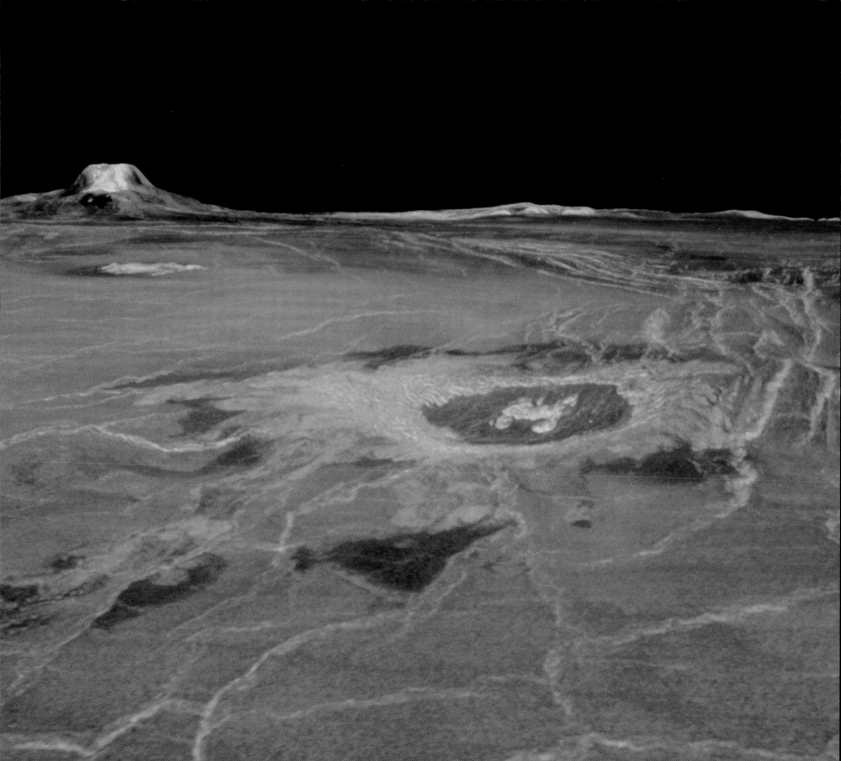

The Innermost Planet

The planet closest to the sun has also had few visitors. No spacecraft has landed on Mercury, and the first probe to orbit the planet arrived in 2011. *MESSENGER* (short for MErcury Surface, Space ENvironment, GEochemistry, and Ranging mission) orbited Mercury more than 4,000 times, depleting its fuel before intentionally crashing into the planet on April 30, 2015.[3]

It took so long to send an orbiter to Mercury for a few reasons. First, Mercury is very close to the sun. A spacecraft traveling there needs to be protected against its heat. *MESSENGER* had a sunshade of heat-resistant ceramic to prevent the sun from frying its instruments. Another reason is that Mercury orbits the sun at a very high speed. On average, the planet is moving at approximately 29 miles per second (47 kms).[4] For a spacecraft to orbit a planet, it needs to match the planet's speed. *MESSENGER* flew in a complex trajectory to build up the necessary velocity, swinging past Earth once, Venus twice, and Mercury three times, using the planets' gravities to speed up.

Once at Mercury, *MESSENGER* made many discoveries, sending back hundreds of thousands of images and collecting data with seven scientific instruments.[5] One of its most significant finds was the discovery of water ice in craters at Mercury's north pole. There, the shadows of the crater walls protect the ice from the sun's searing heat. *MESSENGER* also gave scientists information about the planet's gravity. From those measurements, they found Mercury's core likely has a layer of liquid.

ESA and the Japanese space agency, JAXA, are collaborating on the next mission to Mercury, called *BepiColombo*. They plan to launch two separate orbiters in 2017. One will map the surface, and the other will study the planet's magnetic field. *BepiColombo* is slated to reach Mercury in 2024.

The MESSENGER *spacecraft spent more than four years orbiting Mercury.*

Our Active Star

Missions to study our sun fall into two classes. The first involves space telescopes that take images of our star's changes, studying solar phenomena from a distance. The telescopes detect bright flares of light and material the sun throws from its surface. The second class studies the effects of these solar changes on Earth.

As Solar Probe Plus nears the sun, the star's enormously powerful gravity will accelerate the spacecraft to a speed of 125 miles per second (200 kms).

Earth has a protective magnetic field called the magnetosphere that shields our planet from the particles ejected by the sun. Still, these spewed particles can damage power systems or orbiting satellites, affecting communications and global positioning services. Astronauts in space are also vulnerable. Studying these eruptions can help us better prepare for them.

The telescopes staring at the sun do not simply study our star in visible light—the wavelengths of energy we can see with our eyes. Instead, they focus on light that has more energy, such as ultraviolet light and X rays. This lets them see how energy moves between different layers of the sun and finally erupts at the surface. Earth's atmosphere blocks some of the ultraviolet light and X rays. Sending telescopes into space gives astronomers a unique opportunity to study these types of energy coming from the sun.

In 2012, scientists using space-based solar telescopes found the sun's flares and ejected material are caused by the chaotic nature of the sun's magnetic field. Its magnetic field lines twist, break, and reconnect. This leads to huge blasts of energy and material.

NASA is also planning to fly spacecraft that study the sun from closer than ever before. Its *Solar Probe Plus* is scheduled to launch in July 2018 and approach the sun in 2024. It will orbit our star and

Gorgeous Side Effect

The sun's huge outbursts of particles can damage electronic equipment on Earth. But they can also give us beautiful displays of light called the auroras. Depending on where they are observed, these are known as the northern or southern lights.

Earth's magnetic field traps some of the fast-moving particles, mostly electrons, from the sun. The electrons collide with atoms and molecules in our planet's atmosphere. This interaction releases light, and the color of this light depends on what type of atom or molecule released it. Green comes from oxygen, red from both oxygen and nitrogen, and blue from nitrogen. Other aurora colors come from a combination of those three colors.

occasionally fly as close as 3.7 million miles (5.6 million km) from the sun's surface.[6] This is eight times closer than any other spacecraft has ever flown.

It will fly through the sun's outer atmosphere, called the corona. Even as it passes millions of miles from the star's surface, it will experience temperatures rising to approximately 2,500 degrees Fahrenheit (1,370°C). Such heat requires advanced shielding to prevent the spacecraft or any of its individual instruments from melting. The mission team plans to protect the spacecraft with a 4.5-inch- (11.4 cm) thick sunshield made of a strong material known as carbon composite.[7]

Scientists have begun constructing and testing some of the probe's pieces. Building the spacecraft and protecting the instruments onboard requires cutting-edge technology that has only recently become available. Project Manager Andy Driesman said that *Solar Probe Plus* is "a difficult mission that's been more than 50 years in the making, one that is now achievable thanks to advances in technology, materials, and design."[8]

One of the spacecraft's instruments will collect some of the material it flies through. Sensors will count the different types of particles in the sample. *Solar Probe Plus* will also have a camera that can take three-dimensional images of the material spewing from the sun.

From landing on the hot, hellish world of Venus to testing material the sun blows away, each new mission to the inner solar system gives humans more insight into nearby celestial bodies. Cutting-edge missions will continue revealing the secrets of our closest neighbors in space.

Sampling an Asteroid

NASA planned to send a probe called *OSIRIS-Rex* to a nearby asteroid in 2016. The spacecraft is designed to study the asteroid's surface and composition using five instruments. But the most exciting part of the mission is slated to occur in 2019. The probe's robotic arm will reach out, touch the asteroid, and send a puff of gas to the surface to loosen rocks and soil. Then it will collect some of that asteroid material and stow it in a capsule. A few years later, *OSIRIS-Rex* will head back to Earth, where the capsule will safely land in a desert. Scientists will carefully open it in an advanced laboratory and study the asteroid sample.

FOUR

HUNTING FOR LIFE
ON MARS

M ars has been a major target of astronomers' studies since long before it was possible to send spacecraft there. Among the earliest people to closely study the planet was Italian astronomer Giovanni Schiaparelli, who observed Mars in 1877. He used a new telescope to map the red planet's surface more carefully than had been done before. He saw narrow lines on the surface and called them *canali*, or "channels." Some scientists believed he was referring to artificial canals, like the waterways built by humans in Venice and Amsterdam. People began to talk of a sophisticated canal system on Mars built by the planet's native creatures.

It took many decades for astronomers to find out the truth—although Mars has large canyons and valleys, there are no artificial canals. There is no evidence for life currently existing on Mars. But astronomers now know the red planet once had a thicker atmosphere. Those layers of gas kept the surface warmer. And evidence suggests

The idea of Mars having canals was later disproven when spacecraft actually visited the planet.

Earth versus Mars

Astronomers like to study Mars because it is relatively nearby and has much in common with Earth. But the planets also have key differences.

These differences may provide clues about why life flourishes on Earth and not on the red planet.

	Earth	Mars
Average diameter	7,918 miles (12,742 km)	4,212 miles (6,779 km)
Mass	6.0×10^{24} kg	6.4×10^{23} kg
Distance from sun	1.0 astronomical unit	1.52 astronomical units
Average surface temperature	59 degrees Fahrenheit (15° C)	−82 degrees Fahrenheit (−63°C)
Atmosphere pressure	1014 millibars	Varies from 4.0 to 8.7 millibars
Atmosphere composition (major contributors by volume)	78 percent nitrogen, 21 percent oxygen[1]	95 percent carbon dioxide, 2.7 percent nitrogen, 1.6 percent argon, 0.13 percent oxygen, 0.08 percent carbon monoxide[2]
Moons	One large moon	Two small moons

liquid water once existed on Mars. Cutting-edge spacecraft continue the hunt for answers about Mars's mysterious past.

The First Views

Scientists first tried sending spacecraft to Mars in 1960. The planet is much farther away than Earth's moon, and accurately guiding a spacecraft there continues to be a major challenge even for modern engineers. In the course of two years, the Soviet Union launched five missions to Mars, but they all failed. NASA's second attempted Mars mission, *Mariner 4*, launched in late 1964 and was a success. Both countries have seen numerous successes and failures in the last several decades.

In 1965, astronomers had their first up-close views of Mars when *Mariner 4* arrived at the planet in July. It sent 22 images back to Earth.[3] These pictures showed the planet's surface was heavily cratered, similar to our moon's surface. By analyzing the effects of the Martian atmosphere on *Mariner 4*'s radio signals, scientists were also able to determine the atmosphere's density. Learning about the Martian atmosphere helped scientists prepare for future landing missions.

Starting in 1971, spacecraft began landing on the Martian surface. A sequence of small rockets and parachutes brought the Soviet Union's *Mars-3* down gently, where it began to take the first picture from the Martian surface. But after collecting only 20 seconds of data, the craft unexpectedly shut down and transmissions from it stopped.[4]

Scientists were able to download the part of the first image, but it was very faint and showed little detail. It turned out a dust storm was occurring on Mars at the time *Mars-3* landed. Astronomers think the storm could have blocked sunlight, dimming the image. It also might have caused the communication failure.

Larger Missions

Astronomers' confidence grew as more missions successfully reached Mars. Their goal changed from simply reaching Mars to carrying out detailed exploration of its surface. Mars exploration spacecraft grew larger and more ambitious. Larger spacecraft are more expensive for a few reasons. First, they involve more parts and scientific instruments, all of which must undergo exhaustive testing on the

Early images from the Mariner 4 *spacecraft were hand-colored based on information sent back by the ship's sensors.*

ground before being sent into space. Second, heavier spacecraft require larger, more powerful rockets to launch them.

Carrying out bigger missions slowed the pace of launches to Mars. In the 1960s and 1970s, space agencies launched an average of one or two spacecraft to Mars each year. But beginning in the 1980s, several years passed between launches. Scientists needed to wait for funding, spacecraft construction, and testing before each launch. In addition, each mission lasted for a longer period. The first Mars missions were simple flybys that studied the planet for a few days. Modern Mars missions enter orbit around the planet or explore the surface. These explorations can continue for years.

◢ A Martian Mistake

In December 1998, NASA launched the *Mars Climate Orbiter* (MCO). This project would go down in space exploration history as an embarrassing failure. Everything went according to plan until the spacecraft arrived at Mars. It then swung too low through the atmosphere, damaging the spacecraft. No further signals were received from the ship. Scientists think the MCO then escaped Martian orbit and was lost in deep space.

The error was caused by a simple mix-up. When designing the navigation system, one team used American units of measurement while another used metric units. It was a costly mistake. NASA now has many systems in place to prevent such an error in the future.

Roving the Red Planet

One of the most successful NASA Mars missions has been the Mars Exploration Rovers. These twin spacecraft, named *Spirit* and *Opportunity*, arrived at the red planet three weeks apart in January 2004. Both made it safely to the surface while encased in airbags made of a rugged fabric material called Vectran. This material is stronger than the Kevlar material used in bulletproof vests.

Life Found?

A meteorite found in Antarctica in 1984 has been the center of a debate for decades. Scientists measured the gases in the rock and compared them with measurements made on Mars. The similarities suggested the rock originated on Mars. Experts believe this meteorite, named ALH84001, formed from lava on Mars approximately 4.5 billion years ago.[6] Then, several million years ago, a large asteroid slammed into Mars. The impact blasted debris off the planet, including ALH84001.

In 1996, planetary scientists reported they had found potential fossilized microbes inside the meteorite—the first sign of life from Mars! The announcement made headlines, and it even prompted US President Bill Clinton to address the nation about its significance. However, other researchers soon poked holes in the findings. There is still no definitive proof the structures inside ALH84001 are the remains of living things.

Each rover was designed to explore Mars for three months, but both continued working much longer. *Spirit* roved the surface until becoming stuck in soft soil on April 23, 2009. It sent its last communication to NASA in March 2010. Engineers were unable to reestablish contact, and the mission was declared over. The other twin, *Opportunity*, was still roving across Mars in 2015. It had driven more than 26 miles (42 km) across the red planet.[5] At first, that might sound like a slow pace. Rovers on Mars, however, need to move slowly and cautiously. Getting stuck in a rut could result in the end of the mission. The rovers on Mars take pictures of their environment and then determine the best path toward a destination. Their navigation software is able to intelligently avoid obstacles.

One of *Opportunity*'s most important discoveries came only a few weeks into its mission. The rover spied blueberry-shaped bits of rock. *Opportunity* analyzed the minerals in the rock using instruments, such as a sensor built by planetary scientist Philip Christensen's team, to determine their chemical composition. The team discovered the rock was made of hematite. This gray mineral is also found on Earth, where it almost always needs water to form. The rover also detected the mineral jarosite, which

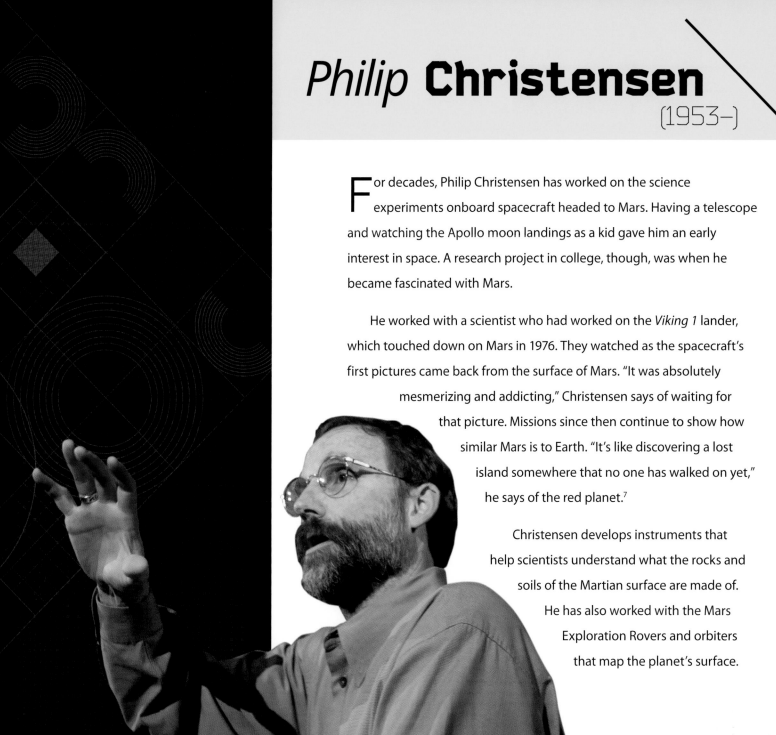

Philip **Christensen**
(1953–)

For decades, Philip Christensen has worked on the science experiments onboard spacecraft headed to Mars. Having a telescope and watching the Apollo moon landings as a kid gave him an early interest in space. A research project in college, though, was when he became fascinated with Mars.

He worked with a scientist who had worked on the *Viking 1* lander, which touched down on Mars in 1976. They watched as the spacecraft's first pictures came back from the surface of Mars. "It was absolutely mesmerizing and addicting," Christensen says of waiting for that picture. Missions since then continue to show how similar Mars is to Earth. "It's like discovering a lost island somewhere that no one has walked on yet," he says of the red planet.[7]

Christensen develops instruments that help scientists understand what the rocks and soils of the Martian surface are made of. He has also worked with the Mars Exploration Rovers and orbiters that map the planet's surface.

43

Why Is Mars Red?

Mars is an orange-red color due to the materials in its surface. Similar to other rocky planets, Mars formed with a lot of iron. Earth was hot enough at its formation for heavy materials, such as iron, to sink to its core. But Mars was not. As a result, much of its iron stayed near the surface and became a component of the planet's rocks and minerals.

When oxygen comes in contact with iron, the two elements interact to become iron oxide, better known as rust. Scientists are not yet sure where Mars got the oxygen to cause this reaction. Some speculate it may have come from the water that likely once flowed on the planet.

can form only in a wet environment. These discoveries provided more strong evidence that Mars once had liquid water on its surface.

In 2012, NASA's Mars Science Laboratory mission landed the *Curiosity* rover on Mars. *Curiosity* is much larger than previous Mars rovers. It is too big for standard landing methods, such as parachutes or airbags. Instead, the mission planners devised a radical new scheme for safely bringing *Curiosity* to the Martian surface. After the spacecraft arrived at Mars, small rockets guided it into the planet's atmosphere. A large parachute deployed to stabilize and slow the spacecraft in the upper atmosphere, but the parachute could not slow it down enough for a soft landing. It detached, and small rocket engines took over. As the lander neared the surface, the section containing the rockets lowered the rover to the ground on long tethers and set it down gently. The rocket module then flew away and crashed at a safe distance. This new landing technique was known as the sky crane. It worked flawlessly.

Since landing in Gale Crater in August 2012, *Curiosity* has been busy. One of its tools drills and grinds rock into powder. Other instruments then study that powder. *Curiosity* detected sulfur, nitrogen, hydrogen, oxygen, phosphorus, and carbon in some of the drilled samples. These are ingredients required for life on Earth. Their presence on Mars hints at the planet's rich, mysterious history.

Curiosity's innovative landing method demonstrated the ability of robotic spacecraft to operate millions of miles from human oversight.

Not Only NASA

Several other national space agencies have launched important missions to Mars. As with the early missions of the United States and the Soviet Union, many of the first attempts were unsuccessful. JAXA sent its *Nozomi* spacecraft in 1998, but equipment failures prevented it from successfully entering Martian orbit. In 2011, China sent its *Yinghuo-1* mission to Mars aboard the same rocket as Russia's *Phobos-Grunt* Mars probe. A rocket malfunction meant the two spacecraft never left Earth's orbit.

India successfully sent a probe into orbit around Mars on its first try. The Indian Space Research Organisation launched its Mars Orbiter Mission in November 2013, and the spacecraft entered orbit on September 24, 2014. From orbit, it studied minerals on the Martian surface and the composition of the Martian atmosphere.

Perhaps one of the most surprising parts of the Indian mission is how inexpensive it was. A minor NASA mission can cost $150 million.[8] A major mission, such as *Curiosity*, can cost $2.5 billion.[9] By contrast, India spent approximately $74 million on the Mars Orbiter Mission.[10]

Cutting-Edge Mars Missions

Mars is a major target for new space missions in the early decades of the 2000s. The ESA planned to send two spacecraft with one launch to Mars for a 2016 arrival, and it is collaborating with Russia for a 2018 mission. One of the 2016 missions will detect gases on the planet, and the other will test technologies needed for future landers. Then in 2018, the two space agencies will launch a lander and rover that will study samples on the surface of Mars. China also plans to send a rover to Mars in 2020, but few details about this project are known, partially due to the Chinese space program's relative secrecy.

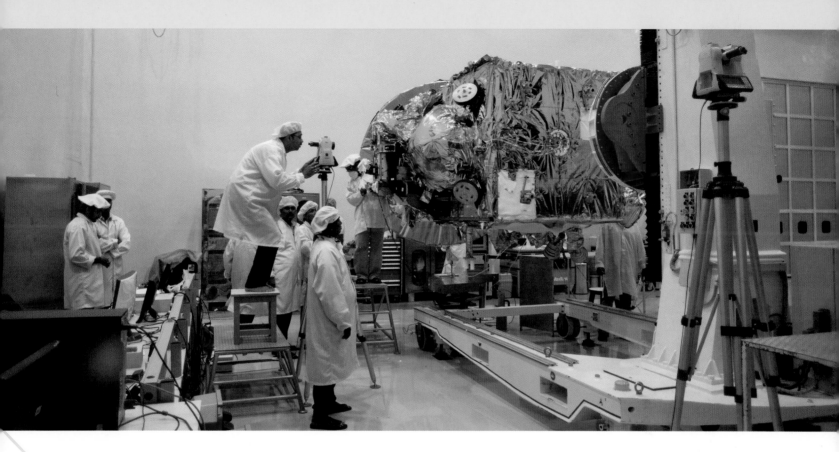

The success of India's Mars Orbiter Mission showed low-cost space exploration missions are more feasible than ever before.

NASA's next planned Mars lander is the *InSight* lander, targeted to land on Mars in late 2016. Its mission is to study the planet's interior, giving scientists crucial clues about how the planet formed.

Following the success of *Curiosity*, NASA announced the Mars 2020 mission. This new rover will use the same complex landing system and a similar body as *Curiosity*, but it will carry more advanced instruments. One of the most exciting instruments is a specialized drill that will collect and securely store samples. Then, a future spacecraft will be able to pick up these samples and return them to Earth for study.

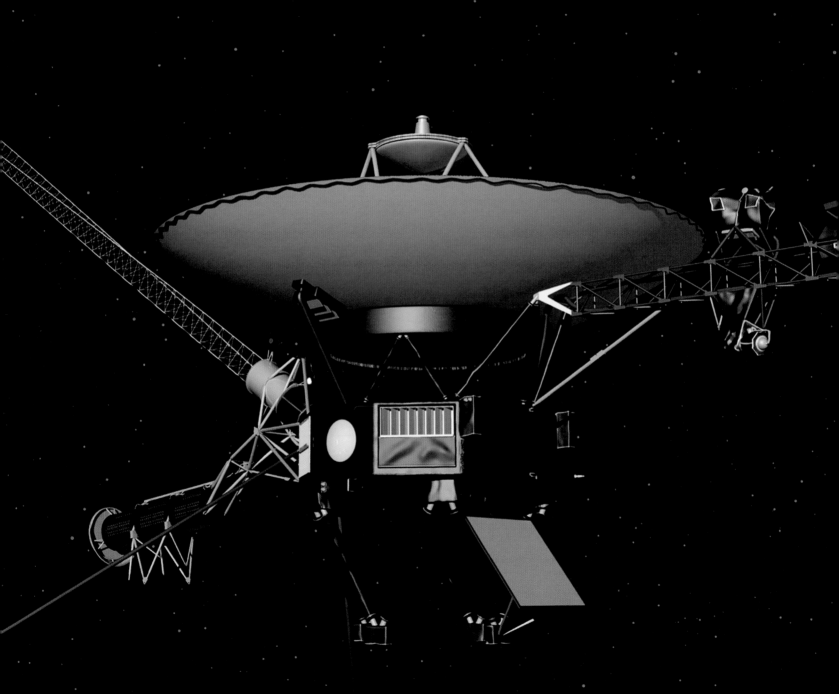

FIVE

TO THE SOLAR SYSTEM'S OUTSKIRTS

As the sun throws off its wind of radiation and particles, it forms an enormous magnetic bubble in space called the heliosphere. The heliosphere encompasses all the planets of the solar system. The outer edge protects the planets from galactic cosmic rays, potentially dangerous energy coming from distant events such as exploding stars. The first spacecraft to exit the heliosphere, *Voyager 1*, left the sun's protective area in August 2012, nearly 35 years after launching from Earth in 1977.

Seven of *Voyager 1*'s 11 instruments were still working in 2015.[1] When scientists saw one of the spacecraft's still-working instruments was detecting more galactic cosmic rays than particles from the sun, they knew the spacecraft had passed out of the heliosphere. *Voyager 1* continues flying through interstellar space and beaming

The Voyager 1 *spacecraft is farther from Earth than any other human-made object.*

Looking for Life around Jupiter

On Earth, life is found everywhere water is found. The first step in locating life in space is to look for signs of water. Evidence from the *Voyager* spacecraft and later probes suggests some of Jupiter's moons may harbor water.

Scientists believe Jupiter's moon Europa may have an ocean beneath its cracked, water-ice surface. NASA's *Galileo* spacecraft, which visited Jupiter in the 1990s, took images of Europa's surface that seem to show moving plates of ice. Astronomers are planning future missions to Europa to figure out how thick this ice shell is, study the oceans, and perhaps drill into the shell and examine the water below. Evidence suggests two more of Jupiter's large moons, Ganymede and Callisto, appear to have liquid water.

information back to Earth. By 2015, it was more than 12 billion miles (19.6 billion km) away.[2] Radio signals from the spacecraft, traveling at the speed of light, take more than 18 hours to reach Earth.

There is a more distant benchmark that *Voyager 1* has not yet reached. It is traveling fast enough to escape the sun's gravity completely. In thousands of years, the pull of the sun's gravity on the spacecraft will be overtaken by the stronger pull of another star. The craft will run out of fuel and electricity long before that happens, leaving it drifting silently through the cosmos.

The Grand Tour

Voyager 1 and its sister probe, *Voyager 2*, carried out the so-called Grand Tour of the solar system's outer planets, visiting Jupiter, Saturn, Uranus, and Neptune. The spacecraft took advantage of a rare alignment of the planets. Astronomers realized if it left in the late 1970s, a spacecraft could use Jupiter's gravity to propel it on to Saturn. It could use the same technique to fling it from Saturn to Uranus and from Uranus to Neptune, dramatically reducing the time it would take to reach the outermost planets compared with a direct flight.

Voyager 1 and *Voyager 2* made important discoveries in the outer solar system. They collected the first evidence that Jupiter's moon Io has active volcanoes on its surface, a feature that scientists, including NASA's Rosaly Lopes, have studied. *Voyager 1* took close-up images of Saturn's moon Titan. The Titan flyby changed the spacecraft's trajectory, flinging it away from the other planets. But *Voyager 2* continued to Uranus and Neptune, becoming the first and only spacecraft to visit these planets. The probe detected ten new moons at Uranus and five new moons at Neptune. It also studied both planets' faint ring systems. It may be many years before Uranus and Neptune are visited again. In 2015, there were no planned missions to these faraway planets.

The Ringed World

One of the most successful spacecraft to explore the outer solar system has been *Cassini*. The probe arrived at Saturn in June 2004. Since then, it has helped scientists measure the masses of several of Saturn's moons, studying whether they might hold liquid seas below their surfaces. *Cassini* has taken incredible images of the planet and its ring system, spotting small boulders that make waves in those rings.

◢ Looking for Life around Saturn

Although the *Cassini* mission spends much of its time orbiting Saturn, it has also flown past many of the planet's moons. The mission scientists think Saturn's largest moon, Titan, has an ocean containing water below its surface. On the surface lie lakes of methane and ethane. Life as we know it could not survive there, but some scientists believe other life forms could potentially thrive. They want to send a submarine probe to swim through these hydrocarbon lakes.

Cassini's up-close photographs of Enceladus found geysers of water and other liquids spraying from the moon's south pole. New research using *Cassini* data shows this moon, Saturn's sixth-largest, has a Lake Superior–sized body of saltwater under the surface.

Rosaly **Lopes**
(1957–)

Rosaly Lopes found the perfect way to combine her love of space and volcanoes. Born and raised in Rio de Janeiro, Brazil, she later studied astronomy at the University of London. She then stayed at the university for her doctoral degree in planetary science and volcanology.

Now Lopes studies the different types of volcanoes that erupt on other worlds in our solar system. In the late 1990s, she was part of the team that discovered 71 active volcanoes on Jupiter's large moon Io.[3] She now works with the *Cassini* spacecraft to study the strange surface of Saturn's largest moon, Titan, including possible ice volcanoes.

Lopes has worked at NASA's Jet Propulsion Laboratory in Pasadena, California, since 1989. She has also found time to give hundreds of public talks about planetary science and write or cowrite eight books.

Cassini *captured stunning images of Saturn's rings, moons, and churning atmosphere.*

It has also mapped the lakes and dunes on Saturn's largest moon, Titan. These dunes are not made of sand, but rather an unknown substance containing hydrogen and carbon. *Cassini* even dropped a lander, called *Huygens*, to Titan's surface in 2005. Both *Cassini* and *Huygens* have shown scientists Titan has an active weather system, like Earth's. The difference is that Titan's is based around methane, whereas Earth's is based around water.

To the Edge

In 2006, scientists launched the *New Horizons* probe on a Pluto flyby mission. When the mission began, Pluto was designated as the solar system's ninth planet. But as *New Horizons* sped toward the tiny, icy world, astronomers decided to reclassify Pluto as a dwarf planet. Several objects similar to Pluto had been discovered in deep space. To prevent the number of planets from increasing indefinitely, astronomers instead created the new dwarf planet designation. Whether it is a full-fledged planet or not, scientists still agree Pluto is an important target.

The *New Horizons* spacecraft spent nine years traveling to Pluto. Only a year after launch, the spacecraft flew by Jupiter and used the planet's powerful gravity to boost its speed. While at Jupiter, the craft tested its instruments, observing the giant planet, its faint ring system, and its moons.

In July 2015, *New Horizons* made it to Pluto. But the piano-sized spacecraft, built to be small and light to permit it to travel extremely quickly, did not have the capability to slow down and orbit the planet. Instead, it would have to study Pluto as it flew past at a speed of approximately 31,000 miles per hour (50,000 kmh).[4] For months before and after the flyby, it was able to collect data. At the time of closest approach, when it passed only 7,750 miles (12,500 km) from Pluto on July 14, 2015, it was able to take images of surface details the size of city blocks.[5]

New Horizons took images of a large, heart-shaped feature on Pluto that captured the public's imagination in July 2015.

◢ Long-Distance Calls

All of NASA's missions use the Deep Space Network for communication between the spacecraft and Earth. Giant antennae located in California, Spain, and Australia provide constant communication, regardless of which side of Earth is facing the spacecraft. Each site has at least four antennae, the largest of which spans 230 feet (70 m) across.[6] The ESA has its own system, called Estrack. It includes ten different stations in seven countries around the globe.[7]

Power Up

Most spacecraft generate power in one of two ways. Some use solar panels to convert light from the sun

into electricity. Others use nuclear power, converting the heat that results from decaying radioactive elements into electric power.

Both *Voyager* spacecraft are fueled by nuclear power. They contain a sample of the element plutonium, which gradually turns into another, lighter element, called uranium. In the process, the material sheds protons and neutrons and gives off heat. Spacecraft components are able to take some of this heat energy and turn it into electricity. The benefit of nuclear power is that it can sustain a spacecraft for decades, even when it is far from the sun's rays. The *Voyager* spacecraft continue to operate long after their launch, and they are projected to remain powered until at least 2025.

Solar power is used only for spacecraft near the sun. Solar panels become less effective at long distances. Spacecraft going to Jupiter or farther typically use nuclear power instead. But for probes exploring the inner solar system, the sun provides a virtually limitless source of electricity.

Messages to Aliens

Both *Voyager 1* and *Voyager 2* have golden discs filled with information, along with the equipment needed to read this information. The discs contain greetings in a variety of human languages, music from different cultures, and more than 100 images representing Earth.[8] It is unlikely the *Voyager* spacecraft will ever encounter alien life, but the messages represent humanity's recognition it may not be alone in the universe.

New Ways to Travel

Spacecraft have a few ways to get to their targets. For decades, spacecraft have used rocket propulsion, which burns a fuel and directs the exhaust backward to thrust the ship forward. Some recent missions are using an advanced new propulsion technology: ion propulsion.

Spacecraft with ion engines use xenon gas as fuel. Magnets and electrically charged components slam electrons into the gas, causing a xenon atom to throw out one of its own electrons. This changes the electric charge of the xenon atoms, turning them into positively charged ions. An ion is an atom that has more or fewer electrons than protons. Magnets then direct these ions out the back of the engine. This results in a tiny amount of thrust to the spacecraft. The force of an ion engine is far lower than that produced by rocket engines. But the ion engine uses its fuel much more slowly. Ion engines can run for weeks or months at a time, slowly building speed. Ordinary rocket engines typically have enough fuel to fire for only a few minutes.

The *Dawn* spacecraft, which entered orbit around the solar system's largest asteroid, Ceres, in March 2015, used ion propulsion to reach its destination. It launched in 2007. Before arriving at Ceres, *Dawn* spent time orbiting another large asteroid, Vesta. Its highly efficient ion engine made this mission possible.

A solar sail is another type of propulsion system. It requires only sunlight to work. Solar sails take advantage of momentum provided by the pressure of the sun's radiation. A large surface can catch this momentum and use it to propel itself forward. In 2010, JAXA tested this concept on the *IKAROS* spacecraft, which flew past Venus. The ship collected light using a solar sail with an area of 2,100 square feet (200 sq m).[9]

A group called the Planetary Society launched a test solar sail spacecraft in May 2015, and NASA is also developing one. At the same time, space agencies are developing more advanced ion engines. Finally, because neither solar sails nor ion engines generate enough thrust to enable the initial takeoff from Earth, engineers are also working to make rocket engines more powerful and efficient. Powerful rockets can lift a spacecraft with a solar sail or ion engine into orbit, and from there the more efficient engine can take over.

Liquid-Fueled Rocket Engine

Liquid-fueled rockets combine fuel and oxidizer in a combustion chamber, creating a controlled explosion. An oxidizer is a chemical that contains oxygen needed for this combustion reaction. Engines on Earth can draw oxygen from the atmosphere, but because rockets operate in space, they must carry their oxygen with them. The force of a liquid-fueled rocket's explosion is directed out the nozzle at the back of the rocket, pushing the craft forward. Liquid-fueled rockets generate large amounts of thrust, but they use up fuel quickly.

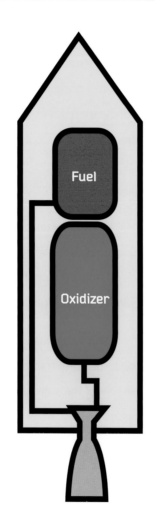

Fuel

Oxidizer

Liquid-fueled F-1 engines were tested on the ground before being used in the Saturn V rockets that sent astronauts to the moon.

Ion Engine

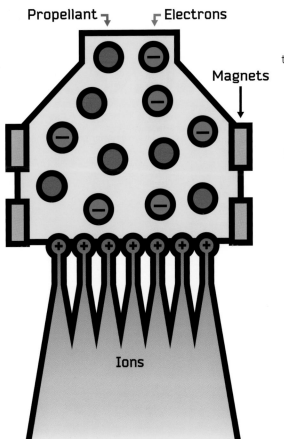

Propellant   Electrons

Magnets

Ions

Ion engines use electricity to generate electrons, which then collide with atoms of propellant. Xenon gas is a commonly used propellant. When hit by an electron, a xenon atom becomes an ion. Magnets force these ions out the back of the engine, pushing the craft forward. Ion engines generate very little thrust. However, they use up propellant slowly, so they can burn for weeks at a time to gradually build up speed.

NASA tested ion engines at the Jet Propulsion Laboratory in California.

SOLAR SYSTEM
EXPLORATION

Planet sizes to scale; distances not to scale.

VOYAGER 1: ENCOUNTERED MARCH 5, 1979

VOYAGER 2: ENCOUNTERED JULY 9, 1979

JUNO: PLANNED ARRIVAL IN 2016

JUPITER

MESSENGER: ARRIVED MARCH 18, 2011

BEPICOLOMBO: PLANNED LAUNCH IN 2017

MERCURY

VENUS

EARTH

MARS

SUN

VENUS EXPRESS: ARRIVED APRIL 11, 2006

MARS EXPRESS: ARRIVED DECEMBER 25, 2003

OPPORTUNITY ROVER: LANDED JANUARY 25, 2004

CURIOSITY ROVER: LANDED AUGUST 6, 2012

MAVEN: ARRIVED SEPTEMBER 21, 2014

MARS ORBITER MISSION: ARRIVED SEPTEMBER 24, 2014

INSIGHT LANDER: PLANNED LAUNCH IN 2016

MARS 2020 ROVER: PLANNED LAUNCH IN 2020

SOLAR PROBE PLUS: PLANNED LAUNCH IN 2018

VOYAGER 2: ENCOUNTERED JANUARY 24, 1986

SATURN

NEW HORIZONS: ENCOUNTERED JULY 14, 2015

URANUS

NEPTUNE

PLUTO

VOYAGER 2: ENCOUNTERED AUGUST 25, 1989

VOYAGER 1: ENCOUNTERED NOVEMBER 12, 1980
VOYAGER 2: ENCOUNTERED AUGUST 26, 1981
CASSINI: ARRIVED JULY 1, 2004

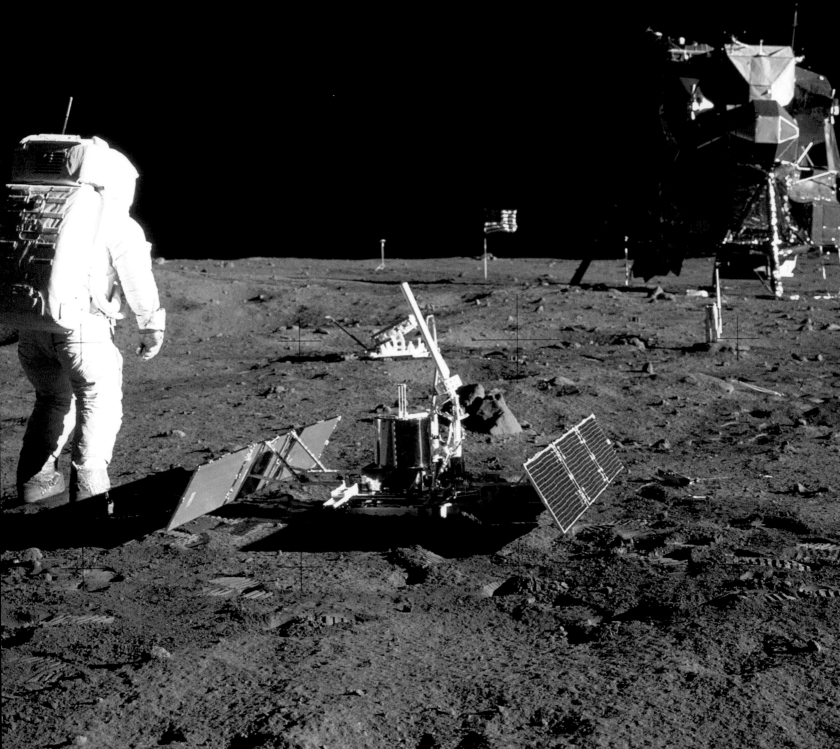

SIX

HUMANS IN
SPACE

Scientists have sent robotic spacecraft to every planet and many smaller worlds in our solar system. In space, robots are easier to work with than humans. Engineers can send robots on a one-way mission, and these spacecraft do not need food, water, or air. They can also handle the extreme environment of space much better than humans can.

So far, human exploration has been limited to orbit around Earth and a handful of trips to the moon. The designers of today's cutting-edge spacecraft are planning for voyages to more distant destinations, including asteroids and Mars. These adventures will test the limits of human technology, skill, and endurance.

By 2016, the Apollo missions to the moon remained the farthest journeys humans had ever taken.

To the Moon

On a hot evening in the summer of 1969, NASA's mission control in Houston, Texas, awaited news from the Apollo 11 mission. Astronauts had just landed their spacecraft on the moon, and 38-year-old Neil Armstrong was preparing to set foot on the lunar surface. His first words from the moon would go down in history: "That's one small step for a man, one giant leap for mankind."[1]

For more than two hours, Armstrong, soon joined by astronaut Buzz Aldrin, collected moon rocks and took photographs of the lunar terrain. They left a few things on the moon: a US flag, a plaque, memorial medallions to the astronauts who lost their lives on earlier missions, and an experiment that let scientists on Earth measure the exact distance to the moon. Then the astronauts lifted off from the moon to meet up with fellow astronaut Michael Collins, orbiting above in the mission's command module. Together, the three astronauts returned to Earth.

The historical lunar landing was driven by competition from the Soviet Union. As part of their rivalry following World War II, the United States and the Soviet Union raced to achieve technological milestones in space.

The race stemmed from political and military tension, rather than from a desire to carry out scientific discovery. Sending spacecraft into orbit required powerful rockets, just like those that could be used to heave nuclear weapons between continents. The space race became a way for each nation to demonstrate its technological and military superiority.

After the Soviets launched *Sputnik 1* in 1957, the space race heated up. The Soviet Union pulled ahead in the early years of the competition. Soviet cosmonaut Yuri Gagarin became the first human in space when he orbited Earth in the *Vostok 1* spacecraft on April 12, 1961. After 108 minutes in orbit,

Space Sacrifices

Animals are the unsung heroes of the space race. Before humans went into space, mission planners sent up many animals to test the environment of space. For example, would the forces experienced during launch be safe for humans? Could a trained animal push buttons and operate switches while in space?

NASA's Mercury program sent up several monkeys and chimpanzees before human astronauts were allowed aboard. The Soviet Union had canine cosmonauts. In fact, the Soviet dog Laika was the first living creature to orbit Earth. In total, approximately three dozen monkeys and chimps and almost 50 dogs have traveled to space.[2]

Sadly, many of the animals died in flight. But their sacrifices made human missions much safer. Many of the animals have been honored since then. Laika, the pioneering canine cosmonaut, has a statue dedicated to her near Moscow, Russia.

the ship automatically fired its engine for reentry and began its descent. During descent, Gagarin felt intense forces resulting from the rapid deceleration of his spacecraft as it descended through the thickening atmosphere. Once the spacecraft was approximately four miles (7 km) above ground, Gagarin ejected the craft and opened his parachute. Both Gagarin and *Vostok 1* made it safety to the ground near Saratov, located in the southwestern region of modern Russia.

NASA's Early Years

The United States first launched a human into space on May 5, 1961, as part of Project Mercury, the nation's first manned space program. Alan Shepard flew into space atop a Redstone rocket in a high arc, though he did not reach orbit. On February 20 of the following year, flying in a Mercury capsule atop a more-powerful Atlas rocket, John Glenn became the first American to orbit Earth.

On the cone-shaped Mercury capsule's wide end was a heat shield to protect the craft and its occupant from the intense heat the capsule would experience while reentering Earth's atmosphere.

Gagarin died in an airplane crash seven years after his historic journey into space.

The sheer speed of a reentering spacecraft compresses and heats up the air in its path, bringing it to thousands of degrees Fahrenheit. Each Mercury capsule used a heat shield made of metal alloys. Subsequent missions have seen this shield improved. The Apollo spacecraft incorporated ceramics and graphite in its shielding. NASA's cutting-edge Orion capsule, which saw its first test flight in 2014, uses a heat shield treated with a synthetic material called Avcoat. The material is designed to burn away as it plunges through Earth's atmosphere, taking away most of the heat while protecting astronauts.

Both Project Mercury and its successor, Project Gemini, demonstrated astronauts were capable of working in space. They laid the groundwork for NASA's moon landing program, Project Apollo. Apollo was enormous in scale, costing approximately $20 billion in 1960s money.[3] This is equivalent to approximately $150 billion in today's money. The Apollo spacecraft included three major parts: the command module, the service module, and the lunar module. The three-astronaut crews on each mission sat in the cone-shaped command module at liftoff. The cylindrical service module, attached to the command module, contained oxygen, water, and other

Women in Space

The Soviet Union sent the first woman, Valentina Tereshkova, into space. She piloted *Vostok 6*, which launched on June 6, 1963. She spent three days in orbit, circling Earth 48 times.[4] Tereshkova had never piloted an aircraft prior to her space flight. But she had experience parachuting, which was a crucial skill for the Vostok missions. After her time in space, Tereshkova earned her doctorate degree in technical sciences and became involved in politics.

The first female US astronaut went to space more than 20 years later. On June 18, 1983, Sally Ride flew aboard the space shuttle *Challenger*. Her mission lasted a bit more than six days. Her second flight, on the same shuttle, launched on October 5, 1984. Prior to submitting an application to become a NASA astronaut, Ride earned a doctorate degree in physics.

supplies. The ungainly lunar module, looking somewhat like a golden spider with a large, silver head, was used to descend to the lunar surface. Its top portion, using the landing legs as a launchpad, rocketed the lunar astronauts back into the moon's orbit. Missions to the moon launched atop the Saturn V rocket, the most powerful rocket booster ever built. A total of six crews landed on the moon. The last, the crew of Apollo 17, returned to Earth on December 19, 1972. Humans have not set foot on the moon since.

Apollo landing crews, including Apollo 17 commander Gene Cernan, left the moon with their suits coated in clinging lunar dust.

Space-Based Laboratories

The next goal for the world's space agencies was to establish a permanent human outpost in space. Aboard this space station, astronauts could conduct scientific experiments and test the ability of the human body to endure long periods of spaceflight. In the future, astronauts traveling to Mars will be in space for years at a time. Spending time in a space station helps scientists and doctors study how living in space affects the body.

The Soviet Union launched the first space station, Salyut-1, in 1971. NASA's Skylab station and the Soviet Mir station followed. The combined efforts of multiple space agencies culminated in the construction of the International Space Station (ISS). This enormous laboratory orbits Earth at an altitude of 250 miles (400 km), circling the globe every 90 minutes.[5] Since November 2000, astronauts and cosmonauts have continuously occupied the station.

It took more than three dozen missions to launch all the pieces of the ISS. The station's first segment was launched in November 1998. The last major piece was finally installed in 2011. As its name suggests, the ISS is a collaboration between many countries. Canada, Japan, and the 22 countries that

participate in the ESA joined NASA and Russia to complete the project.[6] Astronauts and cosmonauts from 15 countries have visited the ISS.[7]

China is not a part of the ISS collaboration. It is working on its own space station. It is called Tiangong, Chinese for "Heavenly Palace." The station is on schedule for a 2022 launch. A test station, called Tiangong-1, went up in September 2011. Tiangong-2 is slated to replace it in 2016. By 2022, the full-scale space station should be operational.

To get their astronauts to these stations, China uses its Shenzhou spacecraft. These spacecraft can fit three people inside, just like the Russian Soyuz. But the Shenzhou program is much newer. Although the first manned Soyuz flew in 1967, the first manned Shenzhou flew in 2003. China has made significant progress in its first years of space travel.

Special exercise equipment is required to make workouts possible in microgravity aboard the ISS.

Harm to the Human Body

It is sometimes said that astronauts in orbit are in zero gravity, but this is not true. Gravity pulls on astronauts in the space station with almost the same force felt on Earth's surface. However, the space station is moving so quickly around Earth that it is in constant free fall, similar to a skydiver. This situation, known as microgravity, allows astronauts to float around as though no gravity were pulling

them down to the floor. Long-term exposure to microgravity can harm the human body. Although it might be fun to float and spin in space, human muscles and bones developed on Earth's surface. The human body works at its best in normal gravity.

In microgravity, muscles weaken and bones can become brittle. After returning to Earth, a person could become more prone to falls and broken bones. The heart can weaken, too. It usually has to pump blood against the force of gravity. But without gravity, the heart does not have to pump as hard. To counteract the negative effects of living in microgravity, astronauts exercise and eat healthy food while in space.

Reusable Spacecraft

One thing the Mercury, Apollo, and Soyuz capsules have in common is that each spacecraft can be used only once. The heat of reentry damages them too much to be used again. The first spacecraft designed to be reusable was NASA's space shuttle. The first shuttle launch came in April 1981, and the last was in July 2011. During the program's 135 flights, the shuttle was used to deploy space telescopes and satellites and to bring astronauts to space stations.

Putting Space Technology to Work on Earth

To send experiments and people off our planet, scientists develop cutting-edge technology. This technology can also be used for many other Earth-based things, including boat safety and medicine.

The last step of each Apollo mission was to deploy parachutes and land the capsule in the ocean. The astronauts would then climb out and sit in a specially designed inflatable lifeboat while waiting for a helicopter to pick them up. NASA developed a special type of lifeboat that would not flip over in choppy water. Although NASA did not need these rafts after Apollo, a similar style of lifeboat is used on thousands of ships on Earth. Researchers believe it has saved at least 450 lives.[8]

More recent NASA research is improving medicine. In the early 2000s, NASA began working with a company called DNA Medicine Institute to develop a handheld sensor that can carry out many tests with just one drop of blood. This rHEALTH sensor checks for hundreds of different molecules that can indicate levels of health or sickness. The sensor is still in testing stages. Soon, though, astronauts will use rHEALTH during flights, and doctors on Earth could use it in remote locations where there are no laboratories.

Once the space shuttle program ended, the only spacecraft able to bring humans to the ISS was the Russian Soyuz capsule. But NASA and private companies are developing new spacecraft to bring astronauts to the ISS and beyond.

Cutting-Edge Spacecraft

Not satisfied with having only one mode of transportation to the ISS, NASA is developing a new crew capsule and a powerful rocket system to loft astronauts to space. These are the Orion spacecraft and the Space Launch System (SLS). The goal is to have both ready for crewed missions in the early 2020s. Orion passed its first test in December 2014 when it orbited Earth twice to check many of its safety systems.

The Scale of Space Exploration

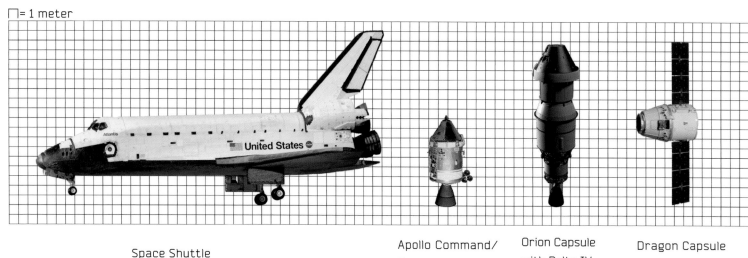

☐= 1 meter

Space Shuttle

Apollo Command/
Service Module

Orion Capsule
with Delta IV
Upper Stage

Dragon Capsule

Orion's crew area, approximately 314 cubic feet (8.9 cu m), or the size of two minivans, can sustain four astronauts with food and other supplies for three weeks.[9] Below the crew is a newly designed service module, which will house Orion's rocket engine. It will also store power for the mission and provide air and water to the astronauts. The ESA is working on this service module.

Before Orion can be used in space, NASA needs a new rocket system that can propel the spacecraft into Earth orbit and beyond. This is where SLS comes in. SLS is slated to be the most powerful rocket booster ever developed, producing even more thrust than the enormous Saturn V. NASA expects to have an early test version, called SLS Initial, ready to fly an uncrewed Orion capsule around the moon

After Orion's first flight test, the flown capsule was brought back to NASA for extensive study.

in 2018. This test rocket will be able to launch approximately 77 short tons (70 metric tons) and produce approximately 8.4 million pounds (37 million Newtons) of thrust at launch. The SLS Evolved rocket, coming a few years after the first version, will

Heavy Launcher

The SLS will not be used only for carrying humans away from Earth. Aerospace company Boeing and NASA expect to use it to launch robotic missions as well. The power of SLS means those spacecraft can get to their destinations much faster than with current rockets. A few possible future targets for the SLS are Jupiter's ice-covered ocean moon Europa, the barely explored planet Uranus, and our searing-hot sun.

be able to loft 142 short tons (130 metric tons).[10] The rocket will use liquid hydrogen and liquid oxygen as fuel.

NASA says the SLS Evolved will be the tool the agency uses to propel astronauts back to the moon and even farther. Plans for the next two decades include journeys to nearby asteroids and eventually a mission to Mars.

Final assembly for the SLS will be done inside the massive Vehicle Assembly Building at the Kennedy Space Center in Florida.

SEVEN

PRIVATE COMPANIES GO TO SPACE

On May 25, 2012, the ISS had a new kind of visitor. Instead of a NASA space shuttle or a Russian Soyuz spacecraft, this one came from a private company. Known as the Dragon capsule, it had been built by SpaceX, based in Hawthorne, California. It did not carry people, but it brought fresh supplies to the station. Six days later, Dragon undocked from the ISS and headed back to Earth for a parachute landing in the Pacific Ocean.

This mission was a game changer. It showed space exploration is no longer just for large government space agencies, such as NASA or the agencies of Japan, Europe, or Russia. Private companies are developing their own cutting-edge spacecraft and rockets.

Space station crews use the ISS's robotic arm to grapple and dock the Dragon capsule.

By 2015, SpaceX had sent six successful uncrewed missions to the ISS. Each has brought scientific experiments, food, and other supplies for the astronauts living aboard the station. Each has returned supplies and waste to Earth.

Both SpaceX and Boeing have partnered with NASA to bring US crews to the ISS by 2017. An upgraded Dragon capsule and Boeing's CST-100 will join Russia's Soyuz in ferrying astronauts between the surface and low Earth orbit.

The CST-100

Boeing has been working on its own spacecraft to carry astronauts. The CST-100 can fit up to seven astronauts, or fewer people and more supplies. The company says the capsule, which looks like a slightly smaller version of Orion, will be ready for flight in 2017. It will bring astronauts to and from the ISS or future space stations.

Most US space capsules have splashed down in water, but Boeing is developing the CST-100 to touch down on land. While traveling through Earth's atmosphere, the craft will release three parachutes. Then, when it is immediately above the ground, it will inflate large airbags to soften the landing. If for any reason a ground landing is not possible, the craft will have the flexibility to also land in the sea.

Reusing Rockets

SpaceX builds more than just spacecraft. It also builds the rockets to launch them. The company's Falcon 9 rocket can carry crewed spacecraft and robotic satellites into orbit. The rocket is divided into two stages. The lower portion is the first stage. It has nine large engines that push the vehicle high into

The CST-100 underwent landing tests in the Nevada desert in 2012.

the atmosphere. After it uses up its fuel, the first stage detaches and falls back to Earth. The second stage takes over, firing its single engine to blast the spacecraft into orbit.

The first stage, with its nine engines and enormous size, is extremely expensive. If it simply falls to Earth, only to sink into the ocean, a new stage must be built for the next launch. SpaceX engineers sought to lower this cost. They figured out a way for the first stage to land itself, making it possible to reuse it. Under this scheme, the first stage detaches when it still has a little

fuel left. As the second stage continues climbing to space, the first stage fires small thrusters to turn itself around. It then uses its main rocket engines to slow down and aim for its landing point. Fins emerge from the stage to stabilize its fall. When it nears the ground, landing legs deploy and the rocket engines fire again. They slowly lower the stage to a gentle landing on a barge at sea.

At least, that was the plan. In early 2015, SpaceX tested its first-stage landing system twice. In January, the rocket crashed onto the landing barge as it descended. Data from the rocket suggested the fluid powering its stabilizing fins may have run out too early. In its second attempt, in April 2015, the system came even closer to success. As it settled on the barge, however, it had too much sideways momentum and toppled.

SpaceX suffered another setback in June 2015. It planned to test its landing system again during a mission to deliver supplies to the ISS. Everything went smoothly for the first few minutes. Its Falcon 9 rocket lifted off successfully, but at an altitude of 28 miles (45 km), the vehicle exploded.[1] SpaceX engineers immediately launched an investigation to figure out what had gone wrong. Though a long string of successful launches may make space flight look easy, it remains an incredibly difficult task.

Heavy Launchers

To launch more weight into space and to send large spacecraft to distant destinations, such as Mars, rocket systems will need to be even more powerful. SpaceX is working on such a system. Its Falcon Heavy is essentially three Falcon 9 rockets strapped together. One is the central core, and the other two are boosters that detach as the rocket rises through the atmosphere.

The Falcon Heavy uses a unique fuel cross-feed system across its three major parts. Fuel from the boosters flows into the central core to power some of its engines during the initial launch. As a result, once the boosters are emptied of fuel and detach, the core is still almost full of fuel for the next part of its journey. The Falcon Heavy is designed to launch humans into space for trips to the ISS and the moon.

SpaceX's long-term goal, however, is Mars. To get to the planet, and to carry people and large quantities of supplies they will need, the company has started developing what it calls the Mars

Colonial Transporter. The head of SpaceX, Elon Musk, wants to set up a human colony on the red planet in case a major disaster, such as an asteroid strike, makes Earth uninhabitable.

A full-scale model of Bigelow's test module was shown to the media in 2013.

Inflatable Space Stations

One private company is working on innovative space stations. Bigelow Aerospace is designing inflatable modules 12,000 cubic feet (330 cu m) in size, approximately the volume of a small house.[2] These structures will weigh much less than standard space station modules, making them easier to launch. The company hopes that, eventually, large space stations could be launched at a fraction of the cost of existing stations.

The company planned to send a small test module to the ISS in late 2015. Once attached to the station, the structure will be inflated. For the next two years, astronauts will occasionally enter the module to take data. One thing they will test is how much cosmic radiation leaks inside this structure. After those two years are up, the inflatable module will be detached and burn up in the atmosphere as it falls back to Earth.

EIGHT

WHERE HUMANS ARE GOING

For the past 40 years, humans have stayed within a few hundred miles of Earth. They've visited the ISS and repaired the Hubble Space Telescope. But now, NASA, other space agencies, and private companies are moving forward with plans to send humans back to the moon, explore an asteroid, and set foot on Mars.

To work toward these goals, scientists and engineers are developing advanced rockets, large in-space habitats to house supplies, and systems to keep humans safe on the flights. Cutting-edge propulsion technologies will enable explorers to fly farther into the solar system.

In the 1980s and 1990s, NASA produced speculative artwork depicting a future Mars mission.

To an Asteroid

If all goes as planned, in the first years of the next decade, NASA will send a robotic mission to a nearby asteroid. The spacecraft will grab a boulder approximately 13 feet (4 m) across.[1] It will then move this small rock to an orbit around the moon. The space agency says it will take six years to complete this phase of the mission.

NASA's planned asteroid mission involves capturing the asteroid in a large bag, then studying it in space.

Once the asteroid and the attached spacecraft are orbiting the moon, NASA will use its SLS to fly two humans aboard an Orion capsule to the boulder. They will dock with the spacecraft. Then, the astronauts will study the space rock for a few weeks. They will also collect samples of the asteroid and bring them back to Earth. NASA says this mission will test technologies needed for trips to Mars.

▴Funding Interplanetary Travel

Today's space travel budgets will not get humans to other planets. For example, NASA's proposed 2016 budget is $18.529 billion.[2] That is approximately 0.5 percent of the overall US budget.[3] At the peak of the Apollo program, approximately 4.5 percent of the nation's budget went to NASA.[4] The high spending was spurred by competition with the Soviet Union. Even at today's reduced funding, the United States spends more money on space than any other country does. But to develop the exciting technology needed to send humans to other planets, people argue much more funding will be needed. The Penny4NASA campaign, launched in 2012, lobbies the government to increase NASA funding to 1 percent of the overall budget, or one penny on the dollar.[5]

The Hazards of Space

Upcoming missions will require humans to venture farther out in space than the ISS and for longer amounts of time. There are many concerns about astronaut safety. The hazardous environment of space is a dangerous place to live and work.

One of the biggest reasons is the electrons, protons, and other particles that zip around through space at nearly the speed of light. Earth's magnetic field protects people on the surface and in low Earth orbit, including those aboard the ISS. But in deep space, these particles can slam into atoms in the human body carrying so much energy they can alter DNA, increase the likelihood of getting cancer, or damage brain cells.

Space shuttle astronauts carefully inspected the underside of their ship for micrometeoroid damage to the heat shield.

Space also has harmful ultraviolet light and even more energetic types of light, such as X rays or gamma rays. To make things worse, the sun unpredictably releases major bursts of harmful light and particles. Luckily, the sun did not let out any major blasts while the Apollo astronauts were in flight. In addition, cosmic radiation was not powerful enough to do much damage during the few weeks they were in space. But Mars is much farther away. Even when Earth and Mars are at their closest, scientists expect the trip to take up to nine months each way.[6]

The travel time in space will be dangerous. The astronauts' spacecraft will need to be heavily shielded. This means extra weight, which also means a larger rocket will be needed. Some scientists are looking into ways for a spacecraft to generate its own protective magnetic field rather than carrying bulky, heavy shielding. Others are studying different types of plastics. Humans living on the moon and Mars for long durations will also need to build bases with extra shielding.

Radiation is not the only hazard in space. Another problem is dust particles, space rocks, and even leftover pieces of old satellites. When moving at high speeds, even a tiny dust particle can tear through a spacecraft wall. The ISS uses a two-layer system to guard against these strikes. There is an outside wall of aluminum and an inner wall of thick Kevlar material mixed with ceramic. A few inches of empty space separates the two layers.[7]

If a dust particle hits the outer aluminum wall, it pierces through and creates a cloud of debris. That cloud expands and disperses its energy over a wider area. Once the debris hits the second wall, the force is not concentrated on one spot, making a puncture in the second wall much less likely.

Advanced flexible space suits will provide much more mobility and flexibility than today's models.

Space Suits

Astronauts wear space suits to protect them from dust and from the pressures and temperatures of space. These have always been bulky. But some engineers, including NASA's Dava Newman, are developing next-generation space suits that will fit close to the human body, making them more flexible. At first the suits will be stretchy. But when worn, the suits will harden against the body, providing pressure to keep the user safe when there is no atmosphere.

This type of space suit will allow the astronaut to move much more easily. This makes it easier to complete complex tasks in space, such as maintaining a satellite or constructing a space station.

Dava **Newman**
(1964–)

Dava Newman has been developing the technology to get humans to Mars for decades. She leads the Massachusetts Institute of Technology (MIT) group working on next-generation spacesuits. Her other research has focused on how the human body reacts to microgravity. And she recently joined NASA as the deputy administrator.

She was only a young child during the Apollo missions, but these early explorations planted a seed in her mind. She studied aerospace engineering in college at the University of Notre Dame. Then, she went to MIT for graduate school. She has two master's degrees in aeronautics and technology policy and a doctorate in aerospace biomedical engineering.

To the Red Planet

One major goal of space agencies and private companies is to land humans on Mars. Getting people to an asteroid or returning them to the moon is a stepping stone on this journey. But this next big step in space will require cutting-edge technology.

With current technology, it will take astronauts six to nine months to get from Earth to Mars. Because the locations of the two planets in their orbits around the Sun dictate when astronauts must launch to efficiently get from one planet to another, humans who set foot on Mars would either stay there approximately one month or 17 months before returning home. The entire mission would take several years.

There is no food on Mars, so astronauts will either need to launch with enough supplies to sustain them for the entire trip or use a supply ship sent to Mars ahead of their arrival. Some scientists think astronauts could create some of the fuel needed to get home from resources in the Martian atmosphere and soil. An instrument flying aboard NASA's 2020 robotic Mars mission will test one such technology.

◢ Mars on Earth

The people who eventually head to Mars will be together for years at a time. They will be limited to a small habitat, and they will have to bring or grow whatever food they need. To prepare for this, scientists have put together a few experiments. Since 2013, the Hawaii Space Exploration Analog and Simulation has had three groups of volunteers live in a closed habitat in a dried lava field on Hawaii. Six people at a time live in a house-sized habitat for a few hundred days.[9] Whenever they leave the closed structure, they must wear an outfit that mimics a space suit. Mars500 was an international project from 2010 to 2011 that locked six men into a mock space habitat in Russia. For 520 days, they lived and worked as though they were in space.[10] Both of these projects help us plan for actual missions to the red planet. The missions provided useful data on the psychological effects of living and working in a small space for a long period.

The atmosphere is much thinner and the force of gravity is much lower on Mars than on Earth. Astronauts would need protection from the low pressure and frigid temperatures on the red planet. They would need to stay within a pressurized habitat or their space suits at all times.

Some scientists are also dreaming of eventually setting up a station on Mars, possibly to serve as a launching point for further exploration. For something like this to be sustainable, though, astronauts will need to find a way to manufacture food and other supplies. Water, used for drinking, growing food, bathing, and other purposes, will need to be recycled. Research for this type of mission is still in its extremely early stages.

The spacecraft that eventually carries crews to Mars will need to be much larger than any flown before.

Getting There

Once powerful rockets launch crewed vehicles into space, the next step is getting to the destination. Rockets produce a great deal of thrust, but their fuel is very heavy, meaning they can only be used for a limited time. Ion engines have the opposite problem. They are highly fuel-efficient, but they produce very low thrust. In either case, missions to distant planets would take an extremely long time. An engine needs to be both powerful and efficient to send a crew of humans, their supplies, and the spacecraft on a long-duration mission.

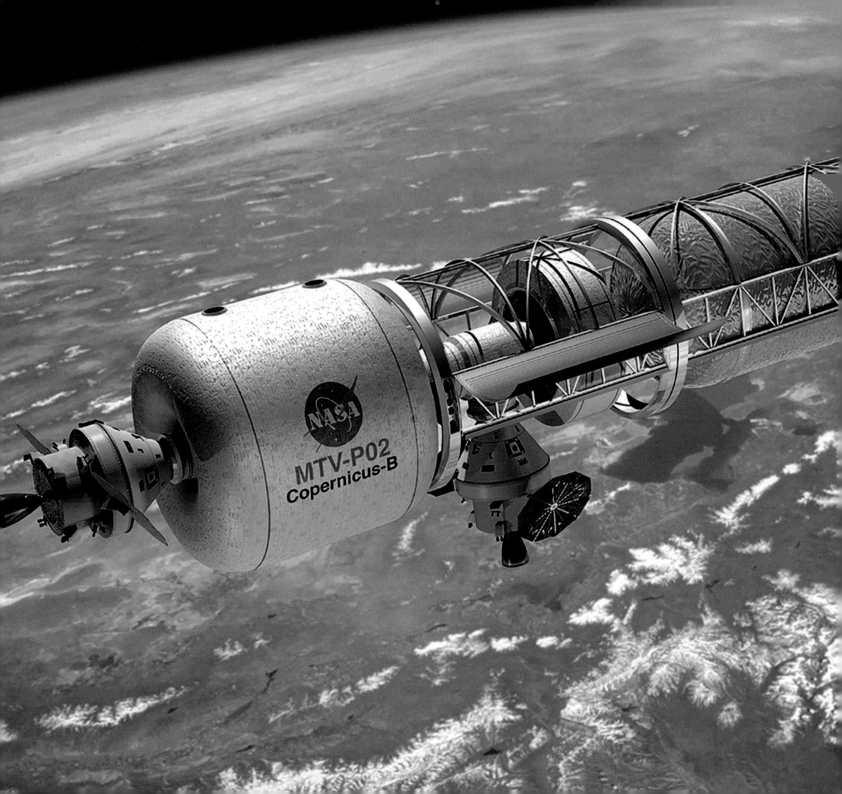

A fusion-powered spacecraft may be the answer. Fusion is the process by which our sun makes heat and light. Light elements, such as hydrogen and helium, fuse together, forming heavier elements. This process releases energy. As of 2015, researchers have not yet figured out how to harness fusion to efficiently generate energy. NASA is researching how this technology might work.

Antimatter-powered rockets may one day make space travel much faster than it is today.

An even more futuristic technology might be matter-antimatter engines. How does this work? Everything you see on Earth is made of normal matter. This can be broken down into the tiny particles, such as electrons and quarks. Scientists know these normal particles also have identical but opposite counterparts. These opposite partners are antimatter.

Physicists can collide miniscule amounts of matter and antimatter in laboratories. When they do, the particles explode and disappear, releasing energy. This energy could propel a rocket forward. But first, scientists need to find out how to safely and easily make, store, and use huge amounts of antimatter.

Pushing the Future

The exciting missions and technology of the future will be enormous in scale and will push the limits of what humans can create. Some robotic explorers will study the surface of faraway planets and moons. Others will scour the surface of Mars for traces of past life. Powerful new rockets will loft humans to a near-Earth asteroid and eventually Mars.

The future promises exciting space exploration missions relying on cutting-edge technology. Both government space agencies and private companies are working to make these missions into reality.

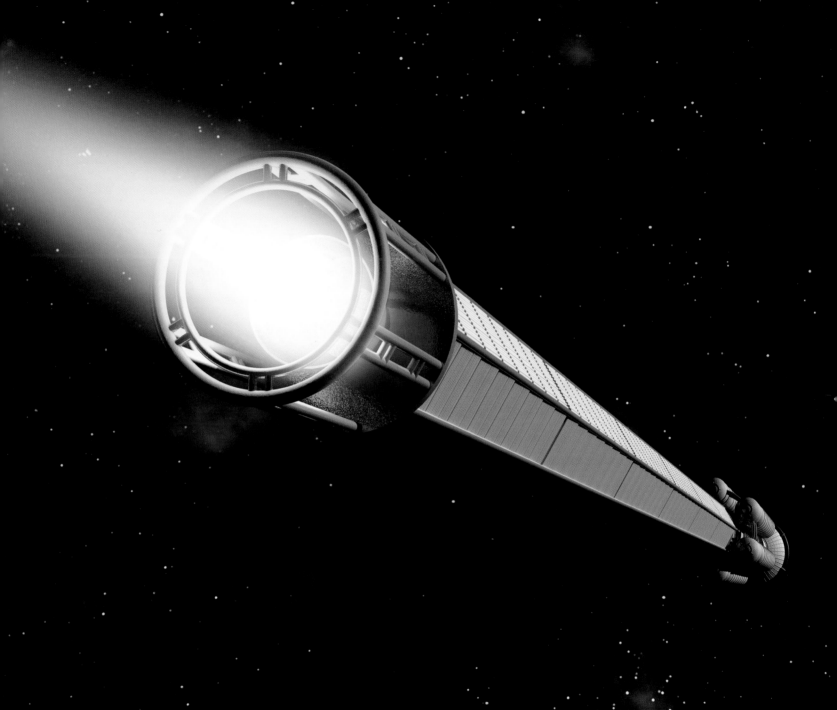

ESSENTIAL FACTS

Key Discoveries

» **Water on the moons of the outer solar system:** Scientists have found signs of water below the surfaces of Jupiter's moons Europa, Callisto, and Ganymede, as well as Saturn's moons Enceladus and Titan.

» **Elements needed for life on Mars:** The *Curiosity* rover detected sulfur, nitrogen, hydrogen, oxygen, phosphorus, and carbon—ingredients required for life on Earth—in Mars rock samples.

» **Inexpensive space travel:** As private companies have entered the space industry, it has become less expensive to construct and launch spacecraft.

» **Space's effects on the body:** The microgravity of space causes human bones to become brittle and muscles to weaken.

Key Players

» **Dava Newman:** Dava Newman is an aerospace biomedical engineer at MIT and NASA. She develops next-generation space suits and studies how the human body reacts to microgravity.

» **Philip Christensen:** Philip Christensen is a planetary geologist at Arizona State University. He develops instruments to find out what the rocks and soils of Mars's surface are made of.

» **Rosaly Lopes:** Rosaly Lopes is a planetary geologist at NASA's Jet Propulsion Laboratory. She studies the different types of volcanoes that erupt on other worlds in our solar system, such as Jupiter's moon Io and Saturn's moon Titan.

Key Tools and Technologies

» **Heavy-Lift Rocket System:** A heavy-lift rocket system produces enough thrust to launch large masses into space and to send spacecraft to distant destinations.

» **Inflatable Space Station Modules:** Inflatable modules will weigh much less than the rigid structures currently used, making them easier to launch.

» **Ion Propulsion:** Ion propulsion is a method to propel a spacecraft by ejecting charged atoms called ions.

» **Reusable Rocket Systems:** Whereas current rockets are discarded, one of these rockets can fire its engines to position itself upright, slow itself, and land softly, allowing it to be reused.

Future Outlook

Although we have not made it more than a few hundred miles off Earth during the past few decades, private companies and governmental space agencies are eager to send humans farther than they have ever traveled. Private companies SpaceX and Boeing, along with NASA, are developing spacecraft to carry astronauts far from Earth safely. NASA plans to send astronauts in the next decade to explore an asteroid. This mission is in preparation for the major goal of both space agencies and private companies: landing humans on Mars. Current plans are for those first steps to occur in the 2030s.

Quote

"[*Solar Probe Plus* is] a difficult mission that's been more than 50 years in the making, one that is now achievable thanks to advances in technology, materials, and design."

—*Andy Driesman*, Solar Probe Plus *project manager*

GLOSSARY

antimatter
Material made up of antiparticles, which have the same mass as normal particles but opposite electric charges.

asteroid
A rocky body drifting through space.

aurora
Lights in the sky formed when particles from the sun hit molecules in Earth's atmosphere.

comet
An icy, rocky object in space that comes from the outer solar system and often produces a tail made of gas and dust when near the sun.

corona
The sun's thin outer atmosphere.

dwarf planet
A space object larger than most asteroids but smaller than a planet.

fusion
Combining two or more things into one; nuclear fusion combines hydrogen into helium and releases energy.

gravity
A fundamental force of nature; the pull between any two things in the universe.

heliosphere

A bubble created by the sun's magnetic field that protects the solar system from energetic particles from space.

hydrocarbon

A compound made entirely of hydrogen and carbon atoms.

magnetosphere

A bubble that protects Earth from energetic particles from space and the sun; it is created by Earth's magnetic field.

orbit

The path an object takes around another object in space, held in place by the larger object's gravity.

radiation

The emission or transmission of energy.

solar sail

A sheet of material that reflects sunlight, which propels a spacecraft.

ADDITIONAL RESOURCES

Selected Bibliography

"Solar System Exploration." *NASA*. NASA, 2015. Web. 18 June 2015.

"Space Science." *ESA*. ESA, 2015. Web. 18 June 2015.

Further Readings

Grayson, Robert. *Exploring Space*. Minneapolis, MN: Abdo, 2014. Print.

Smibert, Angie. *Amazing Feats of Aerospace Engineering*. Minneapolis, MN: Abdo, 2015. Print.

Stott, Carole. *Space Exploration*. New York: DK, 2014. Print.

Websites

To learn more about Cutting-Edge Science and Technology, visit **booklinks.abdopublishing.com**. These links are routinely monitored and updated to provide the most current information available.

For More Information

For more information on this subject, contact or visit the following organizations:

Kennedy Space Center Visitor Complex

SR 405
Florida 32899
866-737-5235
https://www.kennedyspacecenter.com

The Kennedy Space Center Visitor Complex features outdoor displays and exhibit halls showcasing NASA rockets and spacecraft representing the entire history of space exploration.

National Air and Space Museum

Independence Avenue at Sixth Street SW
Washington, DC 20560
202-633-2214
http://airandspace.si.edu

This museum has 21 galleries full of exhibits about the history of flight, the US manned space program, space telescopes, and more.

SOURCE NOTES

Chapter 1. Landing on a Comet

1. Jean-Pierre Bibring. "*Philae*: Reflections and Hopes." *Rosetta Blog*. ESA, 13 Mar. 2015. Web. 10 July 2015.

2. "How Rosetta Arrives at a Comet." *Rosetta*. Jet Propulsion Laboratory, n.d. Web. 10 July 2015.

3. "Fast Facts." *Giotto*. ESA, 10 July 2015. Web. 10 July 2015.

4. "Rosetta Swoops In for a Close Encounter." *Rosetta*. ESA, 10 July 2015. Web. 10 July 2015.

5. "Fast Facts." *Rosetta*. ESA, 10 July 2015. Web. 10 July 2015.

Chapter 2. Entering Space

1. "Les Voyages Extraordinaires." *The Works of Jules Gabriel Verne*. Epguides, 26 June 2015. Web. 10 July 2015.

2. "This Month in Physics History." *APS*. APS, Apr. 2010. Web. 10 July 2015.

3. "Brief History of Rockets." *NASA*. NASA, 12 June 2014. Web. 10 July 2015.

4. "Germany Conducts First Successful V-2 Rocket Test." *This Day in History*. History Channel, 3 Oct. 2014. Web. 10 July 2015.

5. "V-2 Rocket." *National Museum of the US Air Force*. US Air Force, 19 Nov. 2014. Web. 10 July 2015.

6. Ibid.

7. Ibid.

8. "Sputnik Design." *Russian Space Web*. Russian Space Web, 3 Jan. 2015. Web. 10 July 2015.

Chapter 3. Visiting Nearby Worlds

1. "Luna 3." *National Space Science Data Center*. NASA, n.d. Web. 10 July 2015.

2. "Venus Fact Sheet." *NASA*. NASA, 9 May 2014. Web. 10 July 2015.

3. "*MESSENGER* Completes 4000th Orbit of Mercury." *MESSENGER*. NASA, 27 Mar. 2015. Web. 10 July 2015.

4. "Mercury Fact Sheet." *NASA*. NASA, 9 May 2014. Web. 10 July 2015.

5. "Overview of *MESSENGER* Spacecraft's Impact Region on Mercury." *NASA*. NASA, 30 Apr. 2015. Web. 10 July 2015.

6. "Mission Design." *Solar Probe Plus*. NASA, 10 July 2015. Web. 10 July 2015.

7. "NASA Gives Green Light for Johns Hopkins APL to Begin Building Solar Probe Plus Spacecraft." *Johns Hopkins Applied Physics Laboratory*. Johns Hopkins University, 8 Apr. 2015. Web. 10 July 2015.

8. Ibid.

Chapter 4. Hunting for Life on Mars

1. "Earth Fact Sheet." *NASA*. NASA, 1 July 2013. Web. 10 July 2015.

2. "Mars Fact Sheet." *NASA*. NASA, 25 Apr. 2015. Web. 10 July 2015.

3. "The Mariner Mars Missions." *NASA*. NASA, 6 Jan. 2005. Web. 10 July 2015.

4. "Mars 3 Lander." *National Space Science Data Center*. NASA, n.d. Web. 10 July 2015.

5. "Update: *Spirit* and *Opportunity*." *Mars Exploration Rovers*. Jet Propulsion Laboratory, 30 June 2015. Web. 10 July 2015.

6. "The Meteorite." *Lunar and Planetary Institute*. Lunar and Planetary Institute, 2015. Web. 10 July 2015.

7. Philip Christensen. Personal Interview. 22 May 2015.

8. "A Look Back at the Beginning: How the Discovery Program Came to Be." *NASA*. NASA, n.d. Web. 10 July 2015.

9. William Harwood. "*Curiosity* Rover Drives $2.5B Make-or-Break Mission." *CNET*. CNET, 31 July 2012. Web. 10 July 2015.

10. Jonathan Amos. "Why India's Mars Mission Is So Cheap—and Thrilling." *BBC News*. BBC, 24 Sept. 2014. Web. 10 July 2015.

Chapter 5. To the Solar System's Outskirts

1. "Spacecraft Overview." *Voyager: The Interstellar Mission*. Jet Propulsion Laboratory, n.d. Web. 10 July 2015.

2. "Voyager." *Voyager: The Interstellar Mission*. Jet Propulsion Laboratory, n.d. Web. 10 July 2015.

3. "Rosaly Lopes." *Planetary Science: People*. Jet Propulsion Laboratory, n.d. Web. 10 July 2015.

4. "Inside 100 Days to the Historic First Exploration of Pluto, *New Horizons* Set to Deliver." *New Horizons News Center*. NASA, 6 Apr. 2015. Web. 10 July 2015.

SOURCE NOTES CONTINUED

5. "NASA's *New Horizons* Nears Historic Encounter with Pluto." *New Horizons News Center*. NASA, 14 Apr. 2015. Web. 10 July 2015.

6. "70-meter Antenna." *Deep Space Network*. NASA, n.d. Web. 10 July 2015.

7. "Tracking Network Operations." *ESA*. ESA, n.d. Web. 10 July 2015.

8. "*Voyager* Record Photograph Index." *Voyager: The Interstellar Mission*. Jet Propulsion Laboratory, n.d. Web. 10 July 2015.

9. "IKAROS Mission Overview." *JAXA*. JAXA, n.d. Web. 10 July 2015.

Chapter 6. Humans in Space

1. "Apollo 11 Timeline." *NASA*. NASA, n.d. Web. 10 July 2015.

2. "Episode 23: Animals Launched into Space." *Astronomy Magazine*. Astronomy Magazine, 26 Mar. 2014. Web. 10 July 2015.

3. Claude Lafleur. "Costs of US Piloted Programs." *The Space Review*. The Space Review, 8 Mar. 2010. Web. 10 July 2015.

4. "Vostok 6." *National Space Science Data Center*. NASA, 26 Aug. 2014. Web. 10 July 2015.

5. "Where Is the International Space Station?" *ESA*. ESA, n.d. Web. 10 July 2015.

6. "What Is ESA?" *ESA*. ESA, 22 May 2015. Web. 13 July 2015.

7. "International Space Station (ISS)." *BBC*. BBC, 2015. Web. 13 July 2015.

8. "Spinoff 2009." *NASA*. NASA, 2009. Web. 13 July 2015.

9. "Orion Exploration Flight Test-1." *Space Systems*. Lockheed Martin, n.d. Web. 13 July 2015.

10. "Space Launch System." *Space*. Boeing, 2015. Web. 13 July 2015.

Chapter 7. Private Companies Go to Space

1. Melody Petersen. "SpaceX Failure Tests Its Bold Agenda." *Los Angeles Times*. Los Angeles Times, 1 July 2015. Web. 13 July 2015.

2. "B330 Module." *Bigelow Aerospace*. Bigelow Aerospace, 2015. Web. 13 July 2015.

Chapter 8. Where Humans Are Going

1. "Asteroid Redirect Mission." *NASA*. NASA, 7 July 2015. Web. 13 July 2015.

2. "A Bill To Authorize the Programs of the National Aeronautics and Space Administration, and For Other Purposes." *US House of Representatives*. US House of Representatives, 23 Apr. 2015. Web. 13 July 2015.

3. "Historical Tables." *Budget of the US Government*. White House, 2 Feb. 2015. Web. 13 July 2015.

4. Ibid.

5. "About." *Penny 4 NASA*. Penny 4 NASA, n.d. Web. 13 July 2015.

6. "Frequently Asked Questions." *Mars Program Planning Group*. NASA, 10 Oct. 2012. Web. 13 July 2015.

7. "Whipple Shield." *Orbital Debris Shielding*. NASA Orbital Debris Program Office, 3 Feb. 2010. Web. 13 July 2015.

8. Jyoti Madhusoodanan. "Microbial Stowaways to Mars Identified." *Nature*. Nature, 19 May 2014. Web. 13 July 2015.

9. Zak Wilson. "120 Days Down, 120 To Go." *Zak Wilson's Blog*. Hawai'i Space Exploration Analog and Simulation, 13 Feb. 2015. Web. 13 July 2015.

10. "Mars500 Quick Facts." *ESA*. ESA, 1 Nov. 2011. Web. 13 July 2015.

INDEX

About the Author

Liz Kruesi found her love of astronomy and dark skies at a young age, during family trips to the Adirondack Mountains in upstate New York. As her fascination with observational astronomy grew, the Hubble Space Telescope began capturing incredible portraits of the universe. Her interest in astronomy led her to earn her bachelor's degree in physics (with a minor in English) from Lawrence University in Appleton, Wisconsin. She also studied graduate astrophysics at Iowa State University in Ames. Since then, Liz has written about astronomy, space, and physics. She loves to tell the stories of our beautiful universe. She is a contributing editor for *Astronomy* magazine, where she worked for more than seven years. Her articles have appeared in *Discover* magazine, *New Scientist*, and others. She has also won a science writing award from the American Astronomical Society for an article she wrote about black holes. When not talking and writing about science, Liz kayaks, cooks, or spends time with her husband and their adopted border collie mix, Kara.